Be the Best Student!

How to Unlock Your Hidden Potentials for Accomplishment and Performance

Kharisma Khalid

First Published in 2016
Published by SCR Books
Copyright © Kharisma Khalid 2016

All rights reserved.
No part of this book may be reproduced, stored in retrieval system, or transmitted in any form or by any means, electronic, mechanical, photocopying, recording, scanning, or otherwise without the prior written permission of the Publisher or the author. Request to the Publisher or the author should be addressed to kharisma@kharismakhalid.com.

Limit of Liability/Disclaimer of Warranty: While the Publisher and the author have used their best efforts in preparing this book, they make no representations or warranties with respect to the accuracy or completeness of the contents of this book and specifically disclaim any implied warranties or fitness for a particular purpose. The Publisher and the author shall not be liable for any loss or profit or any other personal or commercial damages, including but not limited to special, incidental, consequential, or other damages.

Financial Disclaimer: The advice provided in this book is general advice only. It has been prepared without taking into account your objectives, financial situation or needs. Before acting on this advice you should consider the appropriateness of the advice, having regard to your own objectives, financial situation and needs. Past performance is not indicative of future performance. The author and the publisher of "Be the Best Student!" disclaim all and any guarantees, undertakings and warranties, expressed or implied, and shall not be liable for any loss or damage whatsoever (including human or computer error, negligent or otherwise, or incidental or consequential loss or damage) arising out of or in connection with any use of or reliance on the information or advice on this book, report, or site. The user must accept sole responsibility associated with the use of the material on this book, irrespective of the purpose for which such use or results are applied. The information on this report is no substitute for financial advice.

Illustrations by Kharisma Khalid

For information about special discounts for bulk purchase, please contact Kharisma at kharisma@kharismakhalid.com.

ISBN: 978-1-63227-145-7 (paperback)
ISBN: 978-1-63227-146-4 (PDF e-book)

Contents

Advance Praise	x
Acknowledgements	xi
Foreword	xvii
Preface	xix

Step 1: Learn What You Love — 1
Find Your Passion
Learn The Easy Way
Learned Helplessness
The Six Levels to Learning Easily
Five Elementary Secret to Learning Easily
Reward Yourself for Your Actions

Step 2: Create Your Own Source of Income — 13
The Cashflow Quadrant
Systemize Your Business
Investment Risk Management
The Twenty Idea Method
Focus
The Aunt Jessica Story

Step 3: Associate with The Best People — 25
Market Yourself
Four Ways to Brand Yourself
Choose Your Friends
Establish Rapport
Be A Good Listener
Balloon-Finding in Seminar

Step 4: Be Optimistic — 53
What Is Optimism
Think About the Future
Keep Calm

The Law of Attraction
Change Problem to Opportunity
My Final Year Project Story

Step 5: Practice Self-Confidence   49
What Is Self-Confidence
The Man Who Met John D. Rockefeller
Effects of Self-Confidence
Act-As-If Practice
Kill Fear or Fear Kills
Goal Setting

Step 6: Outperform Your Competitors   61
Competitors Are Inevitable
Your Are Your Own Business
Winners Focus On Winning
Identify Your Competitors
Clarify Your Purpose of Competition
Plan Ahead

Step 7: Be A Lifelong Student   73
Read Books and Listen to Audio Programs
Go to Seminars
What Gets You Here Is NotEnough to Keep You There
The Comfort Zone
The Downfall of Nokia
No One Is Better Than You

BONUS STEP: Express Your Gratitude   85
Develop an Attitude of Gratitude
Always Say Thank You
Commit to Accept Praises with Thank Yous
The More You Give, The More You Will Get
Be Grateful to Yourself
Take Full Responsibility for Your Life

Putting It All Together	97
Bonuses	108
About the Author	109

*For Mom and Dad,
who love and help and assist me
unconditionally in the ups and downs of my life
and who always told me to start writing my own book.*

Thank you!

ADVANCE PRAISE FOR *BE THE BEST STUDENT*!

"Kharisma explains his ideas clearly in his 'Be the Best Student!' book. He describes the methods and ways in this book step-by-step, so that you can just follow it along, use the concepts and see your success at the end of the road."
Raymond Aaron, Canada
New York Times Bestselling Author
The Author of Chicken Soup for the Canadian Soul

"Impressive! You need to have this book in your collection. It's the book for those who wants the best of their lives! This book has the steps and insights that can help and assist you to get to where you want to be in the future. Read it, apply it, and experience it yourself."
Khing Wong, Malaysia
The Author of Hello Entrepreneurs
Malaysia's Creative Business Coach & Top Corporate Trainer

"This book has consolidated the best success formula by many successful people that can change your life! This is a must-read for all pathfinders."
Zayne Ling, Singapore
Author, Ecommerce Startup & Branding Strategist
Entrepreneur and Founder of eCommerce Simply Academy

ACKNOWLEDGEMENTS

While writing this book, I've realized that I've owed the information that I was writing to a lot of people. The good thing was that I realized it early on. Because of the experiences that I had from the moments when I was with them, I got to write lots of them in this book.

First and foremost, I would like to say Alhamdulillah, that is all praises to Allah the Almighty God, for keeping me healthy and well and alive up till the day I've finished writing this book, and for giving me all the resources and the experiences and the insights and the opportunities to be with the people available around me all my life.

I would like to thank my family for their support in me writing this book. My dad, Khalid Andong, my mom, Siti Yati Matori, and my siblings, Kharisna, Khairul Izzati, Mohamad Khairulhidayat, Khairunnadia, and Mohamad Khairunnaim. Without them, this book would never have been possible to start because I would never have a loving family such as them. I would like to thank my paternal grandma, Merdiah Aman, for keeping me well-fed while I was busy wiriting this book, and my maternal grandma, Poniah Gaip, for her support in me writing this book. I would also like to acknowledge my uncles and aunts, Ms. Marsia Matori, Mr. Mat Ponidi Matori, Mr. Marselin Matori and Ms. Samsiah Samsudin, for being patience with me throughout my life in my secondary school years, and Mr. Johari Andong and Ms. Suriati Morshidi, for having me in their house before. Because of them, I got to learn the lessons on action takers.

Kharisma Khalid

Thanks to Ahmad Azroy Shafiq Jamil for giving me the lessons on midsetting as in My Secondary School Years subchapter. Thanks to Muhammad Azzir Maili for giving me the lesson on the ways to treat people. Thanks to Luqmanul Hakeem Mohamed Habibollah for going to seminars with me. Thanks to Mukriz Muzany Mazlan for being my friend who was also together with me during my ups and downs from my secondary school years up till my college years. Thanks to Abdul Hakim Mohamed for being my roommate and my friend during my college years. Thanks to Amirul Hidayat Ahmad for assisting me with lots of things.

Special thanks to Siti Hajar Hamzah, Ainul Filzah Shahidin, Firdaus Rosli, and Sallehuddin Muhammadi Ahmad Hussain, for being my wonderful Final Year Project group members, my friends and for teaching me the lessons in the reality of having group members and in leadership. Thank you to Abdul Hafiz Idlan Mohamad Shuhaimi, Ahmad Ashree Kamarulzaman, Ahmad Firdaus Fakhri Ahmad Radzi, Athira Fauzilan, Latifah Abu Bakar, Mohamad Aiman Iqbal Adnan, Mohamad Hafizi Yusman Yeoh, Mohammad Nor Aiman Noranual, Muhammad Arif Kamarul Azmi, Muhammad Arif Mohammed Khir, Muhammad Faiq Roslan, Muhammad Shafiq Mahbob, Nur Najlaa Baharudin, Nurul Alwani Che Aman, Rosmaelida Mohd Nasir, for being my wonderful classmates and friends throughout my college life.

Thank you to Hafiz Azizi Mohamad Ali, Nurul Huda Mohd. Nizam, Azrul Azwan Mohammad Sani, for giving me the experiences that I needed to learn for the lesson of competition. Thank you to Azim Daniel Husin, Safwan Fikri Tajudin, Mohd. Akmal Osman, Muhammad Helmi Ibrahim, Mohd. Hafizan Huzlan, Muhd. Afif Fizer, Zulfaqar Azrin Zainin, Mohd. Fawwaz Yusri, Mohd. Fariz Nazmi Pozai, Achmed Syukri Mohamed Habibollah, for assisting me during my in-plant training semester.

Be the Best Student

Special acknowledgement to Ms. Safrina Zainal Abidin, for her insights on how other people think about you, as in the subchapter, Clarify your Purpose of Competition, in Step 6. Because of her insights during her training in my class before, I was able to write about it in this book.

Many thanks to my trainers, Mr. Ahmad Hishamuddin Hassan, Mr. Anuar Hasan Hamdan, Mr. Hafiz, Mr. Mohd. Hafiszudin Mohd. Amin, Ms. Nurhayani Romeo, Ms. Haslina, Ms. Raja Norashikin Raja Shamsudin, Ms. Shanaz Ramli, Ustazah Naziefa Mohamed, Ms. Hairun Nisa Daud, Ms. Zakiah Saizan, Ms. Amni Saizan, Ms. Yanti Marliana, Ms. Syazwani, Ms. Nurul Rafidza Muhamad Rashid, Ms. Hazni Yati Mohd. Ghadzi, Ms. Noormelah Shamsul Anuar, Ms. Dahlia Asyikin Ahmad Zainaddin, Ms. Norulmubarakah Ibrahim, Ms. Farah, Ms. Siti Daniah, Dr. Abdul Zubi Ahmad, Mr. Hafiz Razali, Mr. Razali Abu Bakar, Mr. Khairul Safuand Md. Salleh, Mr. Fahrul Rizal Abdul Halim, Mr. Ainul Hazmin Abdul Hamid, Mr. Muhammad Tajuddin Reduan, for training me throughout my college years, and because of their training and guidance, I am able to be the best student I could ever be right now, and I was able to get the Award of Excellence from my college. Thank you to Ms. Jamilah Mohamed Ali and Mr. Mohd. Fairudz Hamdan for allowing me to be on good terms with them and for assisting me to accomplish wonderful achievements throughout my college years. I would also like to thank Ms. Nadiatul Mardhihah and Mr. Mazlan for managing the things related to my Final Year Project, that at last, my group managed to get our project done. Also to Ms. Roslina Aziz for managing the documents related to my in-plant training so that I was able to undergo it hassle-free.

My in-plant-training experience was one of the best experiences that I got from my workplace. So, I would like to thank Mr. Alex Tan Kok Fatt, Mr. Mohd. Fazrul Mohd. Khasim, Mr. Mohd. Hafiesz Mohd. Amir, Ms. Anita Razani, Ms. Hemalatha Segaran, Mr. Mohd. Hafizh Mohd. Hashim, Mr. Syazwan Fahmy Zahar, Ms. Shalini Rajendran, Ms. Munirah Alimuddin, Mr. Vijendran Veeraya, Mr. Hairul Nizam, Ms.

Kharisma Khalid

Zuliana Talsis, Ms. Suriani Mustaffa, Ms. Hanani, Mr. Aminuddin VP Hamzah, Ms. Yusnizah, Ms. Nadia, Ms. Rebekah, Ms. Mastura, Ms. Aminahtulzaharah, Ms. Rosaliza, Mr. Yeow Wei Wen, Ms. Sheila Shamsudin, Ms. Joan, Ms. Putri, Mr. Muizuddin, Mr. Hisham, Mr. Roy Chow, Ms. Suraya, Ms. Tun Noor Shahya, Ms. Bama Karupiah, Mr. Michael, Mr. Abdul Halim, Ms. Azira, Ms. Ranjini, Ms. Noormah Md. Noor, for being the best known colleagues and leaders that I ever worked with. Because of them, I am able learn a lot more things and have a lot more fun than I had just from my years in college, and I was able to pass my in-plant training with flying colors because of their guidance.

My high school years were one of the moments that lead me to my life right now. Thus, I want to acknowledge Ms. Zuraida, Ms. Ramlah Salleh, Ms. Nor Azura Mostapha Nor, Ms. Monaliza Johnwayne, Ms. Nurhuda Ramli, Ms. Noor Ashikin Mohd. Nor, Ms. Hazliawati Hajmi, Ms. Sharifah Hasiah Wan Bujang, Ms. Ainor Afizah, Ms. Norani Padil, Ms. Ivy Mady, Mr. Gahffari Hamdan, Mr. Lastli, Ustaz Azwan Abdul Aziz, Mr. Vincent Nelos Terim, Mr. Shamsul Senusi Jamal, Mr. Abang Zainorin Mohd. Shazli, Mr. Nasarudin Sapuan, Ustaz Fikhrullah, Ustaz Tengku Azhar, Ustazah Sharifah Munah Wan Bujang, Ustazah Normala Hassan, Ms. Saptuyah Gondek, Ms. Marziah Omar, Ms. Masmery Sirat, Ms. Sarimah Anshari, Ms. Nor Zainisham Muhd. Zain, Mr. Zulkiple Che Hasan, Mr. Ya-kub Noh, Mr. Noordin, Ms. Nurmuhaiyun Dzulkifli, Ms. Siti Noorfairuz Serbini, Mr. J Hamzah Shaari, Ms. Norliza Yong, Ms. Nurul Aziatul Akma Hajemi, Ms. Salwani, Mr. Azizul, Mr. Nik Mohd. Azlan, Ms. Nurafida, Ms. Zuliati Sapawi, Ms. Jamilah Mohamed Jamil, Ms. Hamidah Ali, Ms. Dayangku Noraminah Awang Ali, Ms. Norfadilah Mohd., Ms. Fatmawati Sazali, Ms. Aishah, Ms. Zah Abdullah, for being patience in teaching me in all my secondary school life. Also to Mr. Mohd. Jaafar Tubo, Mr. Abang Ramli, Mr. Abdul Razak, Mr. Hamdan, Mr. Budiman, Mr. Amran Muh Amin, for allowing me to be on good terms with them, from my secondary school life and up till now.

Be the Best Student

Lots of thanks to my success, wealth, business, and life skills trainers, Mac Attram, Alex Mandossian, Courtney Smith, Blair Singer, Peng Joon, Jay Abraham, Brian Tracy, Kevin Green, JT Foxx, Larry Loik, Andrew Lock, Sandy Jadeja, and many more amazing teachers from whom I've learned with throughout my life. Without them, I would never advance this much in my life.

Special thanks to Raymond Aaron for his clear guidance so that I could manage to finish writing this book. Also to Liz Ventrella as my Personal Book Architect, for being patience with my questions and works related to finishing this book. Without both of them, I could never have finished writing this book.

Having written that, my thanks and gratitude goes to you, the reader of this book. It is because of your faith in yourself that you took action to buy this book. Everything you do makes a difference in this world of abundance.

Kharisma Khalid

FOREWORD

A young man AWAKENED at his age of 20! For students or parents or anyone who would like their children or themselves to be a REAL successful person from schooling all the way to their future era, this book is very useful, a MUST READ! A step-by-step guide with many successful strategies and techniques that you can practically apply and your life will never be the same again!

Being a seasoned entrepreneur with a Master Degree in Marketing, I have earned extensive international business experience, owning some great international skin care brands and having companies in Hong Kong, Germany and China. In the past years, I've encountered many tough challenges that cost me a fortune and enormous time to turnaround the situations. Then, I realized that what have been taught in my school life was way different from what the real world needs. The main key to success is to have the mindset and skills set just like the successful people have. Kharisma shared his experiences and offered solid facts to back them up in this book! I fully agreed with them and feeling delighted to write this foreword for him.

Kharisma is not from a wealthy family; however, through his keen studying and continuous learning, he is now both an academic-smart while a street-smart young person. Through his realization of what he did in the past and what can be done better plus the adding on what he learned from many well-known global platform speakers, coaches, authors and successful entrepreneurs. He is now sharing what he learned and what he has practiced successfully, so that you can save much time, thoughts, energy or money (through mistakes) for your upcoming wealthy and successful life.

Kharisma Khalid

Earn from your reading!

YOU ARE WHO YOU THINK YOU ARE.

Be a great student and a successful person to be known in the world!

Orpheus Choy
CEO of ONE Concept Group
Entrepreneur, Brand Creator, Marketer and Speaker

PREFACE

Welcome to the best student book. In the pages ahead, you will learn how to be the best person you can ever be in your entire life. You will learn the technique that top performers use to learn easily and well. You will get to know what you can do to create your own source of income so that you can have unshakable self-confidence. You will learn how you can associate with the best people so that they can help you and assist you, and even create the environment where you can get the best out of yourself, as well as much more, in the pages to come.

The Golden Rule in reading this book is: don't believe a word I wrote. Because all of them are based on my own experience, it doesn't make it right or wrong, or true or false. What matters most is whether you apply it at least ten times or not. Why ten times? Because the *80/20 rule* application says that 20% of your actions account for 80% of your results. If it works for you afterwards, keep using it. But if it doesn't, you're welcome to ignore it.

Why Best Student?

All my life, I've been a student, whether I realize it or not, as I keep learning and growing, formally or informally. I keep learning, right up to this moment; I really like to learn something new and interesting and keep getting the "Aha!" moments myself.

From all the books I have read, seminars I have attended, people I have met, talks and audio programs I have listened to, and webinars that I have watched, I came to the conclusion that the ones who lived their lives fully, made more money, had more happiness, had a lot of free time, lived healthier, as well as having other things desired by humans, are the ones who are the best students throughout their lives!

What do I mean by *the best student?* The best students are the ones who are able to unlock their hidden potentials for accomplishment and performance. They are the ones who commit to be and to do the very best throughout their lives. They are the ones who keep learning and taking action to improve themselves from time to time. As the basketball coach, Pat Riley, said, "If you are not getting better, you are getting worse." They don't necessarily score the best grades in their school or college years. They don't necessarily get benchmarked to be the best people in their community. They don't necessarily get ranked to be the highest income earners in the world. They don't necessarily be the top at everything.

Every person who has ever accomplished anything extraordinary has turned out to be the best student throughout their lives, whether it is by trial-and-error, learning from other people, or learning from mistakes made either by themselves or by other people. When you develop yourself to the point where you are the best student you can ever be, your future will be infinite. As JT Foxx, *the World's #1 Wealth Coach,* said, "How you change, is how you succeed!"

By being the best student, you will be able to learn easily and well. You will set bigger goals, dream bigger dreams, and achieve them faster than you ever imagined possible. You will commit to do whatever it takes for you to get something that you want, because you know, by learning and applying what you've learned, you can solve any difficulty, overcome any setback, and achieve any objective you set for yourself. You will make a lot more money than you ever thought possible, by applying the things you have learned throughout your life. You will be around the best people in your field, network with them, and learn from them, as you grow and get along with them.

Be the Best Student

You are a Remarkable Person

You are a remarkable person with unlimited ability. You have the ability to become anyone you want, achieve anything you want, and get anything you want. You can learn anything you can put your mind to. You can dream any dream you want. You can solve any problem you have.

You have all those abilities inside of you. It is your job to unlock it so that you can utilize that potential of yours to achieve your needs and wants.

You are a potential genius. Your brain consists of about 100 billion neurons, each of which is connected to as many as twenty thousand other cells in a complex network. This means that you can obtain and store as much information as you want, have as many thoughts as you can, relate each of them, and make conclusions from them to help you to get to where you want to be in the months and years ahead. You are able to learn anything you want, easily and well. You can score any grades that you want on the tests and exams that you have throughout your life—all by using your very own brain.

Being remarkable isn't always about what others think about you. It is what you think about yourself that counts the most, as that is what decides whether you are able to accomplish something or not.

T. Harv Eker, the writer of the best-selling book *Secrets of the Millionaire Mind,* an amazing teacher of mine, taught his students about the *process of manifestation.* It states that thoughts lead to feelings, feelings lead to actions, and actions lead to results. He tells us that actions are the bridge from your feelings to your results, and that your feelings come from your thoughts. That also means that how you think about yourself affects your feelings, and it will also affect your actions, which will eventually affect your results.

In the pages ahead, you will learn about how you can think greatly about yourself so that it will motivate you to take action to get the result that you want. You will also learn about how you can keep positive most of the time so that your feelings will be up most of the time.

As your feelings are what will decide whether you take action on something or not, it is your job to take control of your feelings and make sure that they stay up for the longest time possible. You, and only you, can control your own feelings.

My business trainer, Alex Mandossian, also known as the King of Electronic Marketing, always said this to his students, *"You are not as good as you think you are. You're better."* He has been training and teaching thousands and thousands of students all over the world each year, and yet, these words of his are some of the words that have changed my life. I was shocked the first time that I heard those words from him, at a seminar that I attended. That was one of the "Aha!" moments that I got from his seminar that will always be useful throughout my life.

From what Alex Mandossian said, it seems that people have only used a bit of their ability, like a drop in the ocean. Thus, whatever you have accomplished up till now is merely a shadow of what you can really do in the future. Your best achievements and happiest moments are still to come.

My Secondary School Years

During my middle school years, my pointers were quite low up till the third year. But, during the third year, I found an amazing friend.

That amazing friend of mine, during his second year, his pointer raised so high, that he got the award as one of the highest pointer climbers in the school.

Be the Best Student

At that time, I was struggling to study for my middle school public exam that would happen at the end of that third year. What was so great about the exam? The thing was, if I didn't pass the exam with flying colors, I wouldn't be able to stay in that school again. I had grown fond of that school, and that was why I wanted to stay in it.

I met him when all of the *third years* in the school were gathered in the library to do exercises on the subject of life skills. He sat right next to me, using the same table as me.

I saw him doing the current exercise easily, and he had scored quite well in the previous exercises we've done in that period. Then I asked him, "How did you do it so easily, and score so well, when I am struggling to do so?"

He said something along these lines, while pointing to some of the images for the questions on his exercise paper, "You know, Kharisma, these are all very easy. They are all based on logic. You see, what is the use of this and this? This is life skills, Kharisma. If you were to use it, how would you? And then, answer it based on your thinking."

"I see. I've always thought that it needs to be based on what I remembered from the books, or what I've learned from the class. I never thought it was based on logic. It never crossed my mind in the first place. But, what if I answered it wrong?"

"Don't worry about answering it wrong, as you will always do so on something you're not very good at. But, you should learn from it, so that the next time you get to answer that kind of question again, you will know the correct answer."

At that moment, I learned three things from him. The first thing was, if I change my mindset, I will change my view of the world. The second thing was, don't be afraid of making mistakes, as it is inevitable. The third thing was, to learn from mistakes.

Kharisma Khalid

The moment that I learned the lessons was the turning point of my life. Amazingly, the next exercise I did, I scored higher than on the previous exercises that I did before I had learned the three lessons. That motivated me to do better in the next exercises. I kept practicing those three lessons.

Since I learned the lesson, my pointer went from 2.86 in the first semester of my third year, to 2.99 in the second semester. I passed my middle school exam with flying colors, and I never thought I could do that!

From the fourth to the fifth year, my pointer went from 3.06, to 3.31, to 3.49, to 3.46. Yes, life has its ups and downs, but that doesn't demotivate me from keeping on.

I passed my high school public exams with only seven As, but it was still great for me, as some of the subjects in which I got A, I've never gotten an A for them before.

My College Years

My college years started when I was 18 years old. As I like computers very much, I enrolled in IT-related courses at my college. Before I entered college, after I had finished my secondary school, I stayed at home and found opportunities to make money online.

One such opportunity was by drop shipping products. I did make some money, but it was not consistent, as it depended on what product I was selling, and the demands of the market for it. Anyway, drop shipping is a way to make money online, literally without the need of capital or stocks to start with, and if you understand its model and how it works, you can start making money right away. I've wrote a report for you if you're interested. Check it out at www.TheBestStudentBook.com via *Dropshipping Report.*

Be the Best Student

Let's get back to the story. After I entered college, I was still doing the online drop shipping thing, but, to my disappointment, I made less and less money each time. I made so little money that I had to put my shame aside and ask for some from my parents. I felt very ashamed of myself. One time, when I was lying on my bed in the college dorm, in the middle of my first semester, I asked myself, "Why did this happen? What did I do that brought me to my current situation?"

After that, I looked for more products that I could sell on the Internet. I kept looking and looking till I found one that resonated with me. Then I found a product that was trending during that time, and I felt the urge to dropship that product instead.

So, I immediately found ways to drop ship that product, and surprisingly, it sold quite well; and by only using that money I made from the first month that I drop shipped the product, I could survive for several months! I said to myself, "Wow! I never thought that I would make this much money in my first month drop shipping this product."

Then, I questioned myself, "What did I do that had brought me to this situation?" I traced it back, and I found one lesson, which was, *sell what my market wants,* and this lesson was in the business area.

From that moment, I stopped asking for money from my parents, my self-confidence increased, and my life in college got better, as I had my own source of income.

During the second semester of my college years, I read a self-help book about how to think like a millionaire. The book was so very interesting and engaging, that I applied the lessons written in it, and my life was never the same again. I learned that the author of the book organizes seminars for the content that he wrote in it.

Kharisma Khalid

During the fourth semester, I signed up for a seminar from the author of that self-help book, and, just like the seminar claimed, that weekend changed my entire life.

Since then, I have met amazing people, I have learned a lot more than I could ever have imagined, I got better and better in my field, I became known more at my college, I learned easier and scored better, and I became the best that I could ever be throughout my college life!

My pointer in college went from 3.69 in the first semester, to 3.78, to 3.94, to 3.92, to 3.90, and finally, to 4.00 in the final semester, after three college years committing to get it!

A Powerful Lesson About Privilege

I once read about a high school teacher who led a simple but powerful exercise to teach his students about privilege. He started by giving each of the students in his class a piece of recyclable paper and asked them to crumple it up. Then, he moved the dustbin to the front of the classroom.

He said, "The game is easy. *All of you* represents the population of the country, and everyone in it has a chance to become rich and move into the higher class. To move into the higher class, all you have to do is to throw your crumpled paper into the dustbin in front of the class while sitting in your current seat."

The students at the back of the class immediately said, "This is not fair!" They could see that the students who were sitting in the front rows had a higher rate of success in doing so. Even with all of that, every student in the class took their shots, and almost all of the students sitting in the front row made it, but only some of the students at the back of the class made it.

Be the Best Student

The teacher ended the game by saying, "Your odds of making the shot increase, the closer you are to the dustbin. This also applies to privilege. Did you realize that only the students at the back of the class complained about this game being unfair?"

"On the other hand, students sitting at the front of the class were less aware of the privilege they were born into. What they could see was only the distance between them and their dustbin."

"Your job is to be aware of the privilege that you have, and use it to do your best to achieve amazing things, while encouraging those who are sitting in the rows behind you to do the same to get the outcome that they want."

People usually take things for granted, including privilege. It was just like the students who were sitting in the front row of the class. What they could see were only the things that they already had. Education is definitely one of the things that is taken for granted by many people. Maybe because they had it since they were little, but a lot more kids and adults in this world wish that they could have the education they desire, like the one that we have right now. So, as Orpheus Choy, the CEO of ONE Concept Group, wrote, "Make the best use of this chance to push yourself up!"

We should be grateful for everything we have been able to get so far. We will get more of what we are grateful for. Here's an example: One of your friends will be having his birthday party next week. You wanted to give him a present, as he is a good friend of yours. So, you put a lot of time and effort in finding the best birthday present for him. You then wrap it up so nicely and beautifully that you were thinking that you would not even want to open the present if you were the one getting it, as it looks too stunningly beautiful. You can't wait for the party that will happen in only a few more days.

Later, on his birthday, you went to his house and gave him the present. When he received the present from you, he then just threw it into his room and went back to enjoy the party. How would you feel? Would you give him a birthday present again next time? This very same thing happens to a lot of people at the receiving end. Because they are not grateful for what they have, they would not get more of it.

The World of Rapid Changes

You now live in a world of where changes happen very fast. What you know today may not be relevant tomorrow. The skills that you have today may be rendered obsolete next month. The job that you have today, you may be laid off from next year. These rapid changes are unstoppable, unavoidable, and inevitable, whether you like it or not.

Albert Einstein was teaching at Princeton University and had just given an exam to a physics advanced class of students. On his way back to his office, the assistant carrying the exam papers asked him, "Dr. Einstein, wasn't this the same exam that you gave to the same class last year?"

Dr. Einstein replied, "Yes, it was."

The assistant then asked, "Excuse me for asking, Dr. Einstein, but why would you give the same exam to the same class for two years in a row?"

Dr. Einstein then simply replied, "The answers have changed."

At that time, in the physics world, with new breakthroughs and discoveries, the answers were changing at such an amazingly fast rate that the same exam could be given for two years in a row and have different answers.

Be the Best Student

Your answers to your own questions are changing faster today than you could ever have imagined before. You probably would not remember what your answers were to your questions, like, "What do I want to do today?" even from last year. The answers have changed so completely, along with the changes that have happened around you, whether you realize it or not.

Harvard University researchers once made three forecasts about the future. First, they said, there will be more change in the upcoming year than ever before. Second, there will be more competition in the upcoming year than ever before. And third, there will be more opportunities in the upcoming year in your field, whatever it is, than ever before. But the opportunities will be different than the opportunities and activities of today.

Those Harvard researchers made these forecasts in 1952. They are as true today as they were then. And today, once again, the answers have changed.

Technologies are also changing more rapidly today than ever before, along with the changes in people's knowledge and discoveries. Just more than a decade ago, people still used film to take pictures. A few years later, the digital camera was introduced; people started to use digital cameras and left film cameras behind.

A few years later, the smartphone was introduced. The smartphone has a camera behind it so that it can be used to take pictures instead of using digital cameras. The camera resolution and quality was then improved upon from time to time. The smartphone was then made with a camera in front of it. And now, the new smartphone has two cameras behind it so that it can take pictures in three dimension and take clearer and more accurate pictures. It happened so fast that you probably wouldn't even realize it, if you didn't take the time to look at it and follow its advancement in the first place.

STEP 1: LEARN WHAT YOU LOVE

Find Your Passion

Perhaps one of the most important things stated in this book is about passion. Almost all people, if not all, who are in the top five percent, or even the top ten percent of their field, are outrageously passionate about what they do. They think about their passion every day, every hour, every minute, and every second. Why is passion that important to them? Here's why:

Passion is one of the most influential motivators of all for those top performers. Passion is what keeps them moving throughout their lives. Passion is what keeps their adrenaline flowing in their blood to keep fighting for it. Passion is what drives them to solve their problems, no matter how hard, how many, or how demotivating their problems are. Passion is what keeps them looking forward to the days, weeks, months, and years ahead. Passion is what keeps them getting up early in the morning and looking forward to what they will be going to do that very day. As Harvey Mackay, the writer of the New York Times bestselling book for fifty-four weeks, *Swim with the Shark Without Being Eaten Alive*, once wrote, *"When you have passion, you speak with conviction, act with authority, and present with zeal."*

Sure, I could go on for a few more pages, but I just wanted to tell you how important and influential having a passion is. You have the ability to be the best student, earn more money, and unlock your hidden potential for accomplishment and performance, if you have a passion for what you do. Here's an example for you:

Let's take a look at one of the world's top earners, Bill Gates, the owner of Microsoft. What is his passion? He is passionate about computers, and, mainly, computer programming. He spent most of his time learning computer programming and programming software. Why? Because he is passionate about it. Because of his passion, he was able to build Microsoft, despite the hardships, negative feedback, arguments, and rejections that he had faced over the years of building it.

How can you find your passion? Start by finding the things that you find easy to learn and easy to do. They are so easy to learn that you don't even remember how you got to learn them in the first place.

Besides that, you can ask yourself this question, from an amazing guru of mine, Brian Tracy, *"What would I dare to dream if I knew I could not fail?"* and list at least ten of them. Then, based on the list you've created, ask yourself this question to each of the things in the list, *"If I only have five years left to live, will I pursue this goal?"* If the answer is yes, circle it, and continue with the next in the list until you've gone through all of them. Then, based on the things you've circled from the list, ask yourself, *"Which one of these will have the most positive effect on my life?"* That one thing, you pursue it as though you've got a gun pointed to your head.

Another idea you can use is to take the job, or goal, that you would take if you were independently wealthy. What would you do if you were extremely wealthy? If you didn't have to worry about making money ever again, what would you do?

Learn The Easy Way

Imagine that you can learn easily and well. Imagine that you don't have to study hard like most people did in their school and college years. Imagine that you can score well on your exams and tests, even without studying hard. Imagine that you only need to learn when you are in your class, or learning or study sessions, and, after those sessions, you are free to do whatever you want. Imagine how your life would be if all those imaginations were your realities. How would your life be different if all those were your reality?

Peter Drucker said, *"The truly educated person today is the person who has learned how to learn continuously and throughout life."* John Naisbitt said, *"The only real skills that matters in the world tomorrow is the ability to learn what you need to know on a regular basis."* T. Harv Eker said, *"Your income can only grow to the extent that you do."* Tom Peter said, *"Continuous learning maybe the only real source of sustainable competitive advantage for individuals and corporations."* All those big names, thought leaders, multi-millionaires, and authors, as quoted, came to the conclusion that learning is very crucial in this ever changing world if you want to survive and thrive. If then, you would rather learn the easy way than the hard way, either way, you still have to learn, right?

How can you learn the easy way? First thing first: you have to learn what you are passionate about. This is one of the ways that I have used throughout my years in college to be one of the top performers in my course. I've been passionate about computers since I was five years old, and I've been learning things related to computers ever since; I've never regretted any of the things I've done related to my passion.

The second way that you can use is to change your mindset. During my middle school years, I had been struggling to score for my middle school public exams, as I found it was hard to learn those subjects, and my semester results were always quite low. Then, I met an amazing friend, who taught me about changing my mindset. Since then, I would be thinking that learning is easy, and I scored quite well in my tests and exams most of the time. Change your mindset, change your world.

The third way that you can use is to find what motivates you to keep learning. When I was in my primary school, there was a primary school public exam held at the end of my primary school years. The result of this exam would decide which secondary school I would be going to, whether it would be an elite school or a normal school. At the start of the final year of my primary school years, my father told me that he would give me a mobile phone if I were to pass the exam with flying colors—Challenge accepted. Since then, all I could think about was getting the mobile phone that I wanted very much; I learned very well, and scored quite well in my monthly exams, and, eventually, I managed to pass my primary school public exam with flying colors—I got that mobile phone.

These are only some of the ways that I suggest. There are many more ways that you can learn the easy way. Your job is to find which way resonates with you, and use it and apply it to your learning so that you can grow much faster, learn more easier, have more time, and learn more things that you are interested in.

Learned Helplessness

I heard a story from my amazing guru, Brian Tracy. He saw it when he travelled to India a few years ago.

When elephant instructors in India catch a baby elephant, they tie one of its legs to a pole with a rope. The baby elephant struggles and struggles, but it can't get free.

For days, the baby elephant pulls and strains the rope. From time to time, however, it learns that struggle is useless, and finally, it gives up.

When the elephant grows up, the instructor keeps it tied to the same pole, in the same way. And, even though it could now easily pull and break the rope and get away, it stands submissively and waits for the instructor to come and get it. It has developed what is called *learned helplessness.*

It has learned that the struggle is useless. As a result of repeated failure experiences early in life, the elephant has learned a self-imposed limitation.

How does this story relate to you? None of us could really escape from the *learned helplessness* trap. We let our past experiences put a ceiling on our future. However, the reality is, there are no limits to what you can achieve except for the limit you put on yourself. You have the ability to achieve extraordinary things, but, if your self-imposed limit is there, it will subconsciously condemn your success. Thus, you have to take the lid off your ability so that you can achieve greater things in your life.

Let me cite you one more example. Brian Tracy once said something like this in one of his seminars a few years back: *"Your life is very much like driving across the country on farm roads. You're trying to make real progress, but you're driving across the country on the farm roads with no road signs and no road maps. You noticed, when you were born, that you don't get any instruction kit, and you have to figure it out all by yourself. You noticed that people lived their lives like backing up in the night and hitting something, and it goes, thump! You get out to see what it is, and it's a new job, or it's a new marriage, or it's an investment, or it's a new business. So, most people drive their lives by watching through their rear-view mirror and going thump, hitting something and getting out to see what it is."*

Because you didn't get any instruction kit for your lives when you were born, you were inclined to do anything, and follow what everyone else around you was doing, in order to survive. Notice that I wrote survive, right there? Yes. Survive. Why survive? Because your brain is programmed to keep you surviving. Its primary job is to keep its owner alive but not to keep its owner successful.

So, because of that, because of your instinct to survive, because of how the reptilian cortex in your brain works, you can't help from getting into the *learned helplessness* trap. It is a matter of fact. You can't change the fact, but you can change your course of action. It is up to you to change it so that you can get over it and move on to create the achievement and success that you desire, which is yet to come and still lies ahead of you. Remember, what you have achieved so far is merely a shadow of what you can do in the future.

The Six Levels to Learning Easily

If you don't know what the stages to learn easily are, you're in for a treat. In this part, I will reveal to you one of the most amazing discoveries ever to occur in the learning arena. By reading, learning, understanding, and practicing the stages below, over and over, you will be able to increase your learning capability by at least a few times. You will be amazed by how much you can learn in a much shorter time frame. You will be able to learn effortlessly. You will be able to have much more free time after your learning sessions. All of these things will happen to you but only when you understand and practice the stages given below, over and over, as though you knew you could not fail.

The first level is *state of mind.* In this level, you have to feel confident, relaxed, and motivated. In order to feel motivated in learning the subject, here are some questions you can ask yourself: What's in it for me? How is this subject related to what I want to do, or be, or have in the future? What will I get if I can understand this subject well? What are the benefits that I will get if I am able to perform in this subject? You will only learn easily and well if you get the benefits of why you are learning it.

The second level is *intake of new information.* You have to absorb the facts that you are learning to suit your specific learning preferences. There are three main learning preferences available for most people—visual, auditory, and kinesthetic. Visual is by what you see, auditory is by what you hear, and kinesthetic is by what you do. Most people only use one way to intake new information. You will be able to learn best if you can combine these three learning preferences. By the way, if you are interested in knowing your main learning preference, you can take the test at www.TheBestStudentBook.com, via the *Identify Your Primary Sense* bonus.

The third level is *subject exploration*. This level requires you to explore the subjects that you are learning. Play around with the new information that you got. Paraphrase it, as T. Smith wrote in his CPA 2012 FAR book, *"Other people's words are never as memorable as your own."* Make mind maps from it. Discuss it with your friends. Sort the information based on logical order. Do the exercises available in the subject, physically if you can. Explore it using all of your three senses.

The fourth level is *remembering the important information.* This level is needed for the information to stay in your brain for a long time. As Brian Tracy said, *"You remember 90% of what you see, hear, say, and do."* As Blair Singer, my trainer, and the writer of the book, *Little Voice Mastery,* said, *"When you look at your notes for a while, after 60 minutes, after 24 hours, after 7 days, and after 4 weeks, your retention rate on it will increase to about four fold."*

The fifth level is *demonstrating that you know what you've learned.* Prove to yourself that you understand the subject that you've learned. Do exercises on it. Test yourself on it. Show to others that you know it. Present to others about it. Teach others of it. Practice it until you've fully mastered it. The final level is *reflecting on how you actually learn.* How well did you learn? Which part is easier for you to learn? Why is that? Which part is harder for you to understand? Why? Feedback is the breakfast of champions. The more feedback you have, the better you can improve next time. The better you can improve, the more easily you will learn.

Five Elementary Secrets to Learning Easily

There are five elementary secrets to learning easily. Why did I write it as *secret*? Because a lot of people don't know about this. Heck, I didn't even know about this until I had read quite a number or books, listened to quite a number of audio programs, and had attended quite a number of seminars on personal development and learning.

The first elementary secret to learning easily is *desire*. You must have the desire to achieve something that you want by learning the subject that you are learning. The subject that you are learning must contribute to the completion of your goals in order for you to learn easily.

The second one is *motivation*. The more motivated you are to learn something, the easier it is for you to intake the new information. You can keep yourself motivated by asking yourself, and answering, the question, *"What's in it for me?"* over and over again. The more you ask yourself that question, and the more answers that you have for it, the more motivated you will be in learning that particular subject.

The third one is *relevance*. The subject that you are, or will be, learning must be relevant to what you want to pursue in the future. The more you focus on learning the subjects or skills that you need the most, in order to accomplish something right now, the faster and easier you'll learn and remember. Choose the courses or subjects that you could use instantly in your current job or to accomplish your current goal.

The next one is *eagerness*. You must be eager to learn the subject that you want in order to learn easily. You must look forward to the learning session. This eagerness makes you think, "I can hardly wait." Always think about how your life will be better if you learned and mastered the subject or skill that you will learn. The more you look forward to the fun of the learning experience and the benefits that you will get from grasping the subject or skill, the more open and confident your mind will be, and the more you will stimulate your ability for learning easily.

The fifth one is *positive expectations*. This means: expecting the better or the best from something that you're about to learn or are learning. T. Harv Eker said, *"Your inner world reflects your outer world."* The more you think better of something, the better it will look in your eyes. The better something looks in your eyes, the more motivated you will be to get it. The more motivated you are in wanting to get something, the more open and positive your mind will be, and the easier and faster you'll learn.

These five elementary secrets are crucial in getting yourself to the state of mind for rapid learning. If you are able to anticipate all five keys to rapid learning, your mind will subconsciously help you to grasp all of the information that you need in order to perform in the specific subject or skill that you are learning, and you will be able to learn all of those things that you want, effortlessly.

Reward Yourself for Your Actions

Nowadays, community teaches us to reward based on results. But seldom, or never, do we hear about rewarding people based on their actions. This is possibly because action is not measurable by other people. What we don't know is that most top performers reward themselves for their actions because they believe that whatever result they got was because they took action on it.

Other people reward themselves based on their results, but you, the owner of your very own bright and successful and unlimited future, should reward yourself for your actions. Here's why:

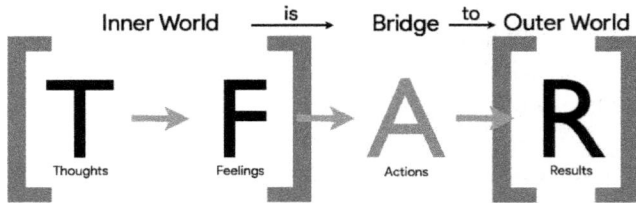

Let's read about T. Harv Eker's *process of manifestation* again. It states that your thoughts lead to your feelings. Your feelings lead to your actions. Your actions equal your results. Actions are the bridge from your thoughts, and feelings, to your results. Results are just the consequences of your thoughts and feelings. Your thoughts and feelings are your inner world, but your actions and results are your outer world. Let me cite you an instance.

Picture yourself thinking of having a goal to make a million dollars within five years. That is a thought. Then, after you think about having that goal, this will bring you to feeling about it. You will then ask yourself, "How will I feel when I make that one million dollars?" Notice how it points you directly to your result? You haven't even thought about your course of action yet!

The next thing that you will think about, after feeling it and envisioning your result, will be your course of action. Your course of action will be the last part, after you have done everything else. Did you notice that you think about your course of action last because it bridges between the inner world and the outer world?

Nevertheless, it happens like that because action is what connects the inner world to the outer world. Your actions materialize as results from your thoughts and feelings. The one thing that you should know right now is that result is just the end point of your process of manifestation. What counts the most are the actions that you take to get to the end point. Is it worth it that you will get the result that you want? Or will you get the result that you want based on all of the actions you've taken in order to get it?

How is this related to this chapter? You see, learning is an action. Action is what we take to materialize our dream. Learning takes a tremendous amount of time, effort, energy, and attention. It requires time to master it. It requires effort to start doing it and keep going. It requires energy to use your brain and your senses for learning. It requires your undivided attention in order to understand it well and to take in the new information.

So, why don't you commit today to reward yourself based on your actions? Only you can measure the quality and quantity of your actions. Be with the top performers in your field—you deserve it; you have the ability to do so; you are a potential high achiever; the seeds of greatness are available in you; and you are incredible.

STEP 2: CREATE YOUR OWN SOURCE OF INCOME

The Cashflow Quadrant

One of the most popular quadrants of all time, related to income generation, is *The Cashflow Quadrant*. It was created by Robert Kiyosaki, the author of the best seller, and number one personal finance book of all time, *Rich Dad Poor Dad*. The quadrant states that there are four ways for you to generate income. What are the four ways?

CASHFLOW QUADRANT

E **EMPLOYEE** YOU HAVE A J.O.B.	B **BUSINESS OWNER** YOU OWN A SYSTEM
S **SELF-EMPLOYED** YOU OWN A J.O.B.	I **INVESTOR** YOU OWN INVESTMENTS

The first way, in the top left of the diagram, is the *Employee* way. This means that these people have a J.O.B. Most top people translate J.O.B. as *Just Over Broke*. Why? Because when someone has a job, most of the time it means that they don't like it. They have to do it from 8 a.m. to 5 p.m. every day, in most cases, except for the weekends, and they only have enough money to get by on, as well as, most of the time, being dedicated to earning money to pay their next bill. In this way, their income has a ceiling on it because they trade their time for their money, and they only have 24 hours in a day.

The second way, in the bottom left, is the *Self-Employed* way. This means that these people are working for themselves. Maybe they work at their own business, or they work on their farm, or they go out selling products to people, just to earn money by themselves, for themselves. Either way, they still trade their time for money. The longer hours they work, the more they are able to earn, but they still have a ceiling to how much they can earn.

The third way, in the top right, is the *Business Owner* way. They are the people who stay in the background of their business. Maybe some of them are the CEO of their corporation or company, but mostly they are the board of directors of that business. They don't have to work for their business. They get other people to work with them. They only have to manage those people, take a look at their business' accounts, and improve their business system once in a while. They have the ability to earn as much as they can, without even having to work in their business, because they created a system for it. What do I mean by system? Read on to know more.

The fourth way, in the bottom right, is the *Investor* way. These are usually the people with money. For these people, their money works for them. Wow! Isn't it great? Typically, they are those who invest in stock markets, businesses, properties, people, and so on. These people have a lot of free time because they don't have to work to get money. Using this method, these people can also leverage their money by using other people's money to increase their profit from their investments.

It is very much recommended for you to take the ways in the right-hand side of the Cashflow Quadrant, because, by using those ways, you will not have a ceiling to how much you can earn, and, more importantly, you will also have all the time you want to enjoy all the money you've made by using those ways.

Systemize Your Business

A lot of people have their own business, company, or corporation, but they work in it. They are the employee of their own business. If they stopped working for their business, that would be it—the business would crumble in no time. By other means, without them, the business would not survive. This means that the owner of the business doesn't have all the time that they want, because they work in their business.

The top people in the business industry don't work *in their business.* They work *on their business.* They have a system to keep the business running without them. What do I mean by system?

A system is a step-by-step process that is repeatable and produces results without the owner working in it. You see a lot of business owners working in their business, but their business would dissolve as soon as they got out of it because they *are* their own business. On the other hand, the high achievers, those who have made lots of money and have lots of free time, *work on their business,* which also translates to *"works on their system."* As Brian Tracy said, *"Every minute you spend in planning saves 10 minutes in execution; this gives you a 1,000 percent Return on Energy!"*

Having a system is what keeps those high achievers out of their business and still able to make lots of money. This is what keeps their business running and improving all the time. Having a system is what distinguishes between regular and wealthy business owners.

How do you create a system? Here's one way that you may use to do so. First, list all of the required tasks that you need for your business. Maybe it's in marketing, accounting, or production—it's up to you. Second, describe the criteria of each task and how to do it. For marketing, how do you want it to be done? After accounting is done with their task, what do they have to do? Third, describe the criteria of people needed for each task. What are the requirements that you want them to have in order to work on your specified task? How much are you going to pay them if they are going to work on the task that you'll give?

Fourth, arrange each task in a list, based on their priority. If possible, combine several tasks together so that you can save the time and capital needed to find those people for the tasks. Perhaps marketing is your first priority. Put it at the top of your list. Then, if production is your second priority, put it second on the list. Fifth, create a main process flow chart, where all of the tasks are combined in the one flow chart, and create a specific process flow chart for each of the tasks. The main process flow chart should show you how each of the tasks relates to each other, and each of the task process flow charts is only for the specific task.

Sixth, get people to work on each task. Explain to them about their tasks, and what they need to do in order to get them done, by briefing and explaining to them about the process flow chart for their task. Seventh, test your system to make sure it produces results, and continues to improve them, in a timely manner so that it will improve the outcome. Nothing works the first time. So, never think that the first time you create your system will be the last time that you'll do so; improvements will always be needed, as we live in a world of rapid change. Remember, what works today, may not work tomorrow.

Investment Risk Management

The great thing about investing is that sometimes you don't have any competition for it, like in a business or a job. You can have a lot of free time if you do this as your main way to make money. You can even leverage your investment by using other people's money so that you

Be the Best Student

can maximize your profit from it. Despite those positive and intriguing benefits of investing, there's a catch behind it. What's the catch?

The catch is that you have to learn to manage the risk in your investment. Why? Because investment requires you to put your money at stake. Then, the market will decide whether you have profit or loss. Right? Wrong! You are the one who will be able to decide whether you will profit or loss from your investment. You just have to learn about it first, before you can master it. That's why the best students are able to make a lot of money—because they learn and master something first before they do it.

I'm not writing this to teach you how to invest. You can learn that from a lot of other books and courses. What I'm here to write about is how you can manage your risk in investment. A lot of books and courses tell you the techniques on investing, but a lot of them also neglect the part on risk management in investing.

The *Law of Investing* states that you have to investigate before you invest. Investigate thoroughly before you invest. Commit to only taking honest, real, and unarguable facts about the investment scheme in which you're going to invest. Since you have taken a tremendous amount of time, effort, and energy to earn that money of yours, you might as well take the same amount of time, effort, and energy to investigate the scheme that you're going to invest in.

The first point under the *Law of Investing* is: The only thing easy about money is losing it. Picture it like this: you have to work hard for thousands of hours of time, energy, and thought, just to get that money of yours. You might even have put in your sweat and tears just to make money. You possibly have to go through all of those just to earn it. And yet, to lose it is very simple. Just invest it carelessly and you can already say "bye-bye" to it. The moment you lose your money, you will never get it back.

The second point is: Don't lose money. This point was made by Marvin Davis, who is a self-made billionaire. He said it during his interview with *Forbes* Magazine when he was asked about his rules for making money. *"Don't lose money."* If you're in doubt about something related to money, go back to the point, *don't lose money*.

The third point is: If you think you can afford to lose a little, you're going to end up losing a lot. I heard quite a similar quote from my trainer, Mac Attram, the world's leading business and personal growth expert. He said, *"How you do anything is how you do everything."* This is very true and much related to this third point. If you do something just how you want to do it, you will do the same for every other thing.

The fourth point is: Only invest with the experts who have a proven track record of success with their own money. Why would you want to invest in someone who doesn't? It doesn't make sense. Yet, quite a number of people still do that. A proven track record of success is required so that you can trust someone with your money to minimize your risk of losing it.

The Twenty Idea Method

If you don't have a business or investment already, fret not, as you can find one that suits your passion, interest, and desire. First, choose whether you want to build a business or an investment. If you decided to choose building a business as your path, ask yourself, "If I were to commit to building a business, what kind of business would I want to build?" Or, if you decided to choose investing your money as your path, ask yourself, "If I were to invest my money in something, which product or scheme, or company or market, would I choose?" Secondly, you will list at least twenty answers to your chosen question on a blank sheet of paper, with the question written in bold, underlined, and capital letters on the top of your paper. If you're interested, there is a business model called *drop shipping* where you literally don't need capital to start doing it. Check it out at www.TheBestStudentBook.com, via the *Dropshipping Report* bonus, to see if it fits you.

Based on those twenty ideas that you've listed, select only one that resonates with you the most. It can be something that you have passion about. It can be something that you're already really good at. It can also be something that you understand the most. It's up to you. If you feel that none of those twenty ideas you have listed resonate with you, you can still add more ideas to the list. List twenty more ideas using the same sheet of paper or using other paper. Then, repeat the same steps until you know what you want to do.

After you figure out what you want to do, commit to do it for at least twelve months in order to see the results. Again, nothing works the first time. Most people stop taking action even before they have started. Why? Because they think about it too much. They think that it will not work. They think about what other people will think about them. They are afraid of failure. They are afraid of rejection. Even after they took action on it for the first time, they stopped doing so afterwards because it was not working for them. It's still just the first time!

Most people do that, but not you dear high achievers of tomorrow. The eleventh president of India, APJ Abdul Kalam, said, *"If you fail, never give up because F.A.I.L. means First Attempt in Learning." "End is not the end, in fact E.N.D. means Effort Never Dies." "If you get no as an answer, remember N.O. means Next Opportunity. So let's be positive."* Henry Ford once said, *"Whether you think you can, or you think you can't—you're right."* It all goes back to how you think about yourself. I heard a story from Andrew Lock, the owner of the website, *HelpMyBusiness.com*, when I was attending one of his seminars.

He said something along these lines, *"Taking action is like pushing a big boulder to the other side of the hill. First, you have to push the* boulder up to the top of the hill. By this, you are exerting your resources in order to achieve your goal. If you stopped halfway, the big boulder will go back down to its starting point and maybe crush you in the middle, and you have to start again from square one."

"Because you are pushing a big boulder, you can't see the top of the hill in front of you, which is your exact stop. It is the same thing as your goal. You can't see where and when you can stop. What if the hilltop is only a few steps away when you stop taking your actions, and the boulder goes back to its starting point afterwards?"

Focus

Focus is what differentiates between normal people and extraordinary people. Focus can be described as undivided attention and courses of actions aimed to accomplish a specific goal. Focusing your actions to accomplish a specific goal is like pouring them down into a funnel, with your goal at the bottom of it. The more actions you put into the funnel, the more the funnel will be filled, and the faster you will achieve your goal.

The *Law of Accumulation* states that every great financial achievement is an accumulation of hundreds of small efforts and sacrifices that no one ever sees or appreciates. This relates fairly well to focus. It shows that great accomplishments are done with focus. Without focus, it is like having a rocket, with two exhausts, destined for the moon—one pointed to the bottom and one more pointed to its side. When the rocket is launched, the rocket will go round and round without ever reaching its destination.

When you focus on your goal, you will be able to reach it faster than before. When you put your undivided attention on your destination, you will get to see it vividly. By focusing on your purpose, you will be able to realize what you can have, before you have it. Focus increases your chance of getting on the highway to success.

Be the Best Student

Let's think about a magnifying glass for a moment. On a sunny day, when you put a paper on the ground, and hold a big magnifying glass a few inches away from the paper, in a while, if it is hot enough, the paper will start burning from the light that is magnified from the magnifying glass. How is this related to focus?

What I want to relate right here is that the magnifying glass focused the light and heat energy that it got from the sun, to its focal point on the paper. If the heat and light energy from the magnifying glass is dispersed, instead of being focused, on the paper, will the paper get burned?

Nevertheless, you can stay focused if you can measure your progress. How can you measure your progress? Start by listing every action you need to take in order for you to reach your goal. Commit to do only those actions, single-mindedly, each time until you've reached it. Remove the roadblocks that prevent you from getting on the highway to success, by continuing to move forward and finding ways to eliminate them.

When I was in semester five of my college years, I had to do a Final Year Project in my course. This project would determine whether I could advance to the final semester or not. Even so, I still had to attend classes and do assignments during that semester. Thus, I could only work on the project on weekends. Every weekend, I'd work on the project and committed to finish it as soon as possible. But, as I could only do it on weekends, I couldn't focus single-mindedly on it. Every time I was continuing that project, I had to recall what I had learned so far during the previous weekends. It was quite tiring for me as I had to recall, and sometimes redo, it all over again, just to remember how the structure of that project was.

Don't let this happen to you. It will be much easier for you to complete your goal if you focus on it rather than not. If you chase two rabbits, both will escape.

Kharisma Khalid

The Aunt Jessica Story

There once was a couple. Let's call them John and Mary. John was working as a plumber, while Mary was working in a supermarket. At the end of every month, they had very little money left, and they were worried about their financial situation all the time. They recycled their kids' clothes so that they didn't have to buy new clothes each time. They got broken bicycles from the junkyard, and repaired them for their kids to ride, as they had no money to buy new ones.

Nonetheless, they didn't worry about it because they knew that when their Aunt Jessica died, they would be rich. Aunt Jessica had said that they were her favorite family members of all and that she would leave everything she had to them when she died. They had Aunt Jessica and she was very wealthy. So, they just stayed at home and thought about what they would do after Aunt Jessica died. Because of what Aunt Jessica had said to them, they treated Aunt Jessica with great care.

However, John and Mary were now in their mid-thirties, and their financial situation was still as bad as ever. They asked themselves, "What if Aunt Jessica lives for another few decades?" They realized that if that happened, they would have to wait for all their lives. They were so shocked to realize their reality that they committed to get out of their financial difficulties as soon as possible. John borrowed some money from the bank, using his house as collateral, and bought a cleaning franchise for his family. John got his children to help him run the franchise and asked Mary to do the accounting. Twelve months later, the franchise was thriving! Then they decided to buy another franchise.

After their second franchise was doing quite well, both John and Mary decided to quit their job. They bought another franchise, and, for the next fifteen years, they bought a franchise every year. By the end of the fifteenth year, they had about 150 people working for them, and their net worth was over a million dollars. They managed to tackle their family's financial difficulties forever!

They were now in their early fifties when they got the sad news that Aunt Jessica had died. A few days later, they had a family gathering for Aunt Jessica's will reading. Most of the family members were in their forties and fifties. The lawyer then read the will, and, to the family's surprise, Aunt Jessica had died broke. In fact, she'd been broke for years. She had been living off her loans. She had mortgaged her house. She'd been living off her family members. She hadn't had any money for years. All of the family members' jaws dropped by what they had just heard.

It was discovered that Aunt Jessica had privately told each of her family members the very same thing as she had told John and Mary. But, as for John and Mary, they were already financially free. They didn't care about Aunt Jessica's will anymore. The other family members, however, were still in the same situation that they were in two decades ago. Their life portion had largely disappeared while they were busy dreaming and waiting for Aunt Jessica to die.

What is your *Aunt Jessica*? What keeps you from taking action in order to chase your goal? What keeps you dreaming that someday you will get the wealth that you want, without ever needing to take action for it? What is your *Aunt Jessica*?

STEP 3: ASSOCIATE WITH THE BEST PEOPLE

Market Yourself

You are your own product. You are responsible for your own exposure. You are responsible for how people think and talk about you. You are responsible for your own marketing. No one but yourself will do it for you.

When you are able to market yourself to suit your preference, your environment will change dramatically. The people around you will treat you how you want them to. You will be able to be around the people that you desire to be around. You will get to be in excellent context for your growth. And most significantly, you will be able to associate with the very best people that you can.

What is marketing? Marketing is where you get people who desire, need, have a use for, and can afford your product or service, to raise their hands in response to your efforts. While selling is on a one-to-one basis, marketing is selling on a one-to-many basis. Marketing is exposure. Marketing is about getting people to know, realize, and be aware of your product or service.

Maybe you've heard the phrase, *"Content is king."* Yes, it is true. Content is definitely the king. You might be the most intelligent and brilliant person in your community. However, if you don't market yourself, no one will know about you; if they don't know about you, you will have no exposure; and your chance for doing something that you want to do with your ability, is downright almost zero. As my trainer, Peng Joon, the author of the bestselling book, *How to Build a*

Money Machine, said, *"Content is king, but marketing is queen, and she runs the house."*

Before you start to market yourself, you have to plan it first. Every minute that you spend on planning, saves ten minutes of your execution time. Firstly, question yourself: What do you want to gain from this marketing effort of yours? Are there any specific reasons for why you want to market yourself? You will not do anything well if you don't see any point in why you're doing it in the first place.

Then, who is your target market? Who do you want to know about you? Who do you want to be recognized by? Describe them demographically and psychographically. List everything that you know about your target market, if possible. Gather only absolute truth about your target market. As the time management specialist, Alex McKenzie, said, *"Errant assumptions lie at the root of every failure."*

Next, after you've identified your target market, what do you want to be known as? How do you want people to think about you? How do you want people to talk about you? What do you want people to know you for? How do you want them to treat you? What do you want to be well-known for?

Afterwards, what can you do to market yourself and to get your target market to think, talk, and treat you the way you want them to? Maybe you can do it just like JT Foxx said, *"Work till you no longer need to introduce yourself."* In my college years, what I did was to utilize the power of word of mouth as my marketing method. I behaved in the way in which I wanted the people around me to think and talk about me. As a result, they did think and talk about me as I wanted them to, and they even talked to their friends and colleagues about me. You can do the same too.

Be the Best Student

Four Ways to Brand Yourself

What is branding? Branding is what other people think about you. When you are able to make people think about you the way that you want them to, your credibility around those people will intensely increase, and you will look amazing in their eyes.

There are four ways you can use to brand yourself in the presence of your target market. By using these ways, you will save lots of time and money on figuring them out by yourself, and the elite people globally use these same methods to brand themselves. In fact, I learned about this from one of the world's top success coaches, and also my teacher, Raymond Aaron.

The first way to brand yourself is branding by *wow*. This way requires you to create a wow impression on your target market. One of the best examples that I've ever seen in my entire life was the *Shamwow* TV commercial, directed by Vince Shlomi, who is better known as Vince Offer. The ad is very impressive in that every time I watched it, it impressed me and made me say "Wow!" I encourage you to watch it to get the idea yourself.

Although *Shamwow*'s ad is very interesting, there are many other strategies that you can use to create that wow impression that you want to have on other people. What I've used is: When I meet and greet people in seminars or social events, and they ask me what it is that I do, I reply with, "I am the president of my own personal services corporation." I get the wow impression from them most of the time. As a matter of fact, it made them remember my name right through to the end of the seminar or social event. It works for me most of the time. How about you?

The second way to brand yourself is *branding by achievement*. When I was in college, I branded myself by getting the best result for the semesters in my course at my college. As a result, I was acknowledged as one of the best students in my course, and at my college, where I got the Award of Excellence. It doesn't have to be something big for you to brand yourself using this method. It only needs for you to have something that you can be proud of, and something that other people can acknowledge you for.

The third way is branding by *testimonial*. Testimonial is a statement from a person about a product or service, or about another person. A testimonial can be done by anyone. The more credible a person is, the more influential will the person's testimonial be. But, do take note, never lie in your testimonials. Never make fake testimonials. Commit only to having genuine, reliable testimonials for branding yourself. Why? Because, when you lie, people will know that you lied. If people know that you lied in your testimonials, they will brand you as a liar instead. You won't want that to occur to you, right?

The fourth way is branding by *association*. When you associate with the best people, you will be able to brand yourself by your association with them. When people see you socializing together with the best people, they will think that you are with them. If they think that you are with them, they will think that you have the same status and ability as them, and they will categorize you in the same category as them.

Choose Your Friends

Jim Rohn, America's foremost business philosopher, once said, *"You are the average of the five people you spend the most time with."* Successful people know about this all along, and that's why they only associate with likeminded people. Successful people always want to be around people who share the same goals, have the same things, have the same way of thinking, and have the same abilities as them. Successful people choose carefully who they want to associate with because they know the reality is what Jim Rohn said.

Be the Best Student

The former First Lady of the United States, Eleanor Roosevelt, said, *"Great minds discuss ideas; average minds discuss events; small minds discuss people."* Henry Thomas Buckle, the English historian, said, *"Men and women range themselves into three classes or orders of intelligence; you can tell the lowest class by their habit of always talking about persons; the next by the fact that their habit is always to converse about things; the highest by their preference for the discussion of ideas."*

Five years from now, your income will be the average of your five best friends. Thus, who do you want to associate with? Who do you want your friends to be? How much do you want your net worth to be five years from now? How do you want to feel when you associate with the people that you choose?

Now that you've decided to associate only with the people of your choice, what can you do to choose them and associate with them? There are several questions that you can ask yourself to help you answer this question. The first question is: "What is my goal?"

The second question is: "What are the criteria of the people whom I want to associate with?" List the answers on a blank sheet of paper with the question at the top of the paper.

The third question is: "What do I want to achieve by associating with them?" Is it for their network? Is it for their contacts? Is it for the environment that they're in? Is it for their energy? Or is it for their context?

The fourth question is: "Why do I want to associate with them?" The bigger the why, the easier the how. The more reasons you have to get something, the easier it will be for you to do the actions related to having it.

The fifth question is: "Where can I find those people?" Can it be in certain clubs? Can it be at charity events? Can it be in certain organizations? Cast a wide net. Fish where the fish are. Be a hunter rather than a farmer. Find rather than wait. Normally, the best people like to be in clubs and charity organizations where they can contribute as much as possible by using their abilities. Just look at Bill Gates. How much of his wealth has he given out for the purpose of doing charities?

The sixth question is: "How can I associate with them?" The best people don't just associate with anyone. They are very picky on who they want to associate and be with because it will affect their lives and their future. Think about what would happen if you associate with problematic people who always complain and badmouth other people, earn little money, and are negative about everything? Chances are, if you are with them long enough, you will become just like them.

Establish Rapport

Perhaps the most important thing in socializing is establishing rapport. What is rapport? According to Nicholas Boothman, the author of the book, *How to Make People Like You in 90 Seconds or Less*, rapport is the establishment of common ground, of a comfort zone where two or more people can mentally join together. Rapport creates the feeling of *"I like and trust this person."* When two or more people establish rapport, their movements, their attitude, their voice details, their body language, and their slang, will subconsciously synchronize with each other. Just visualize what would happen if you were living in a foreign country with a lot of foreign residents around you, but, then, you find someone who is from the same country as you. Chances are, both of you will become best friends in no time—and that is rapport in action.

When you establish rapport, people will help you as though you have already been friends with them for a long time. When you establish a common ground with people, they will like you and trust you, and want to work with you. When you make people like you, they will want to help and assist you, if you ask them for it. The higher the quality of rapport you have with them, the more they want to cooperate with you. If you can master the skill to establish rapport with anyone, your future will be unlimited.

Here is the step-by-step system that you may use to establish rapport with the people that you want to know. Read it, understand it, practice it, learn more about it, and use it to open your path to success.

Step one is to have *appeal*. To make the best impression on someone, there are three things that you have to fulfil. First, you have to look good. People do judge a book by its cover. Second, you have to sound good. Develop a pleasing tonality or voice to appeal to auditory people. Third, you have to feel good. You radiate the energy that you have to the people around you.

Step two is *The Effective Communication Formula*. The formula consists of three parts. The first part is to know what you want. If you don't know what the point is of what you are doing, you won't be able to do it well. The second part is to find what you want. Do everything in your power to get what you want from your conversation. The third part is to change what you do until you get what you want. Always improve your method of communication in order to obtain your desired goal.

Step three is your manner of *greeting*. Greet them openly. Make eye contact. Smile. Be the first to say, "Hi!" Lean towards them to show your interest in them. These are ways to show them that you are friendly, approachable, and "open for business."

Step four is *establishing rapport*. Become synchronized with their movements and their primary sense. Have the same attitude, make the same movements, and speak the same way as they do. This step enables you to empathize with the other person, and to make you feel what they feel. By the way, if you're interested in identifying your primary sense, you can take a test at www.TheBestStudentBook.com, via *Identify Your Primary Sense* bonus.

Step five is the art of *conversation*. This step consists of two parts: Part one is that of talking. People like to talk about themselves, so spend more time asking about them than you spend talking about yourself. Part two is that of listening. Show them that you are interested in them. Make a genuine effort to engage with what the other person is saying and feeling.

Be a Good Listener

To be a good listener, you have to show that you are honestly interested in the other person. You cannot fake this, as the other person will know whether you are sincere or not. When you fake this, it will be shown in your body language. The key to being a good listener is by making a genuine effort to engage with what the other person is saying and feeling. To put it in another way, it is an active effort to get and recognize the information and emotions of what is being said by the other people.

The quieter you are, the more you are able to hear. With that being said, what is the difference between listening and hearing? Here's an example: Picture a baby crying. If you hear it, you can only hear the sound of the baby crying. But, if you listen to it, you will be able to get the meanings behind the cries of the baby. You will also be able to get the underlying feelings behind the baby's cries if you listen actively to it. That's why some mothers know what their baby wants just from listening to their cries.

The truth about listening is that you will be able to learn more if you listen more. Therefore, listen more than you talk. I heard a proverb before that said something along these lines, *"Your idiocy reveals itself when you talk too much."* For me, this is quite true. When you talk too much, the tendency for you to show that you don't know something is quite high. However, when you listen more, you are not revealing anything. In fact, you will be able to learn something instead from the person who does the talking.

When you listen more, you will be able to learn more. When you listen more, people will like you because they like a person who is interested in listening to their stories. People like to talk about themselves. When you listen more, you will be able to get the meanings and feelings behind the other person's words. When you listen more, the self-esteem of the other person increases, making them feel great, hence making them want to be around you more. Make people feel great, and they'll remember you throughout their life. As Carl W. Buehner said, *"They may forget what you said—but they will never forget how you made them feel."*

You can start to listen more by asking questions. As Rudyard Kipling said, *"I keep six honest serving men (they taught me all I knew); their names are What and Why and When and How and Where and Who."* Practice starting your conversation by talking a bit about yourself, and then ask the other person questions about themselves.

Your aim in listening is to empathize with the other person as much as possible. You can show how much you get from listening to the other person by paraphrasing what they have said. When you do this, you will make them feel that their words are very valuable and important. This increases their self-confidence, and they will thank you by their actions towards you later.

When you are listening, firstly, you do this attentively without interruptions. Listen calmly and patiently without responding. Nod, smile, and agree with them while you are listening. Next, pause for a few seconds before replying to their questions or statements. This makes the other person feel that their words are important. Then, question for clarification. Ask questions that makes them explain more about what they've just said. Lastly, paraphrase their words. Ask for clarification from them. If you can do this, just like what the other person means, they will be very flattered.

Balloon-Finding in Seminar

I once read a story about a group of a hundred people in a seminar. In one of the sessions, while the speaker was speaking, he suddenly stopped and decided to do an interesting activity. He asked the audience to enter a room filled with white balloons.

He started by giving each of the seminar participants a balloon. Then, each of them was asked to write their name on their own balloon using a black, bold marker pen with a chisel tip. Afterwards, all of the balloons were collected and were put into the next room, which was empty.

Then, all of the participants were told to enter that room and were asked by the speaker to find which balloon had their name written on it, in ten minutes. Everyone was frantically searching for their balloon, colliding with each other and pushing each other aside, and, for a moment, there was absolute chaos in that room.

When the ten-minute balloon-finding activity ended, it was discovered that no one was able to find their own balloon. Next, each of the participants was asked to pick a balloon randomly from the room and give it to its owner. In a few minutes, everyone had their own balloon back. What was the goal of the activity?

The speaker continued his speech. "This is exactly what happens in our lives. Everyone is frantically looking for what they want, without knowing where it is, and without even helping each other to get what they want."

Be the Best Student

"However, if everyone helps each other to get what each of them wants, everyone will eventually get what they want much sooner. If you help others to get what they want, they will help you to get what you want. Give them what they want, and you will get what you want. This very same thing applies to the networking concept. If you don't network, chances are, you won't be finding the help that you need all your life."

This is closely related to associating with the best people. Have you ever wondered why the best people always get what they want very quickly? The very reason for that is because they understand the value of networking. Your network is your net worth. The more people you network with, the higher your chances will be of getting the help that you want. You will reach your goal faster, and your rate of success will be higher.

By networking with people, you will be able to achieve more than you ever thought before. By networking with people, you will be able to perform better, since you will have the confidence that you can accomplish anything that you want from your network.

Commit today to associate with the best people. Market yourself to get more exposure. Brand yourself in the way that you want people to think about you. Choose who you are friends with, since your income will be the average of your five best friends in the next five years. Listen attentively and flatter people when they talk, and network to increase your net worth.

STEP 4: BE OPTIMISTiC

Congratulations on reading up to the middle of this book! Or, did you? Anyway, in this section, you will get to know what the best people do to stay in a good mood most of the time. You will read what the meaning of optimism is, and how to apply it in your daily lives. You will learn why keeping calm is crucial for your accomplishment and performance. I will explain one of the best laws ever discovered in the success arena, which will be able to save you money, get you more results, and work for you, if you persist in using it long enough and understand it clear enough. This law is also used by the maximum achievers. You will read about this, and many more things, in the pages to come.

What is Optimism?

Optimism means to be hopeful and confident about the future or the positive results of something. Optimism is about thinking positively and confidently about what is yet to come. Optimism includes the thinking that you are responsible for everything you do and everything you have and get.

Optimism is a state of mind that is positive and where a person thinks and feels that they will get the best in whatever things they do. An optimistic person will confidently think that they will get a positive result in the things that they put a lot of effort into it. An optimistic person will be responsible for everything that happens to and around them. And they are offensively positive, because they know that if they think positively and act positively, they will get positive results.

Nevertheless, what is this positive thinking all about? How is it related to success? What can you do to stay optimistic? Being optimistic is easier than most people think. This is because our mind can only hold one state at a time, whether it is positive or negative. When you dwell on positive outcomes all the time, what will you get? Of course, you will get positive outcomes. It is much easier to *be* optimistic if you *stay* optimistic. If you keep going back and forth from being positive to being negative from time to time, it is like going back and forth from one place to another from time to time. But then, yes, it is much easier to stay in one place at a time.

When you think optimistically, your life will be showered with positive thoughts and amazing opportunities to achieve your goals. You will be able to see the opportunities that you couldn't see before. You will live your life and hunt your desires as though you know you cannot fail. You will do whatever it takes to get something done, without worrying about what other people think of you, because you know that you are the best person that you can be. You will keep chasing your dream from day to day as though there were no tomorrow, because you can see your future so vividly and so closely to you, that it is within your grasp.

Staying optimistic is easier than starting to be optimistic. It is said that you need ten units of energy to get started, but you need only one unit of energy to keep moving. To stay optimistic, you must do what the optimists do most of the time—commit to taking full responsibility for your own life. Only think about positive and empowering thoughts all the time. Think about the future rather than the past. Drive your car looking through the front window rather than the rearview mirror, and observe how your life changes for the better.

Think About the Future

The world belongs to the future thinkers; and the future belongs to the competence of these thinkers. Optimistic people think about

Be the Best Student

the future. They are a future thinker in that they don't worry nor think much about their present. They still think about their present, but they aim for the future. They usually have a clear vision of what they want to be, and have, and do in the future. They are normally a person with nicely developed patience, but they don't tolerate time wasters. For them, their future life is everything and it will determine their value and worth.

If you observe and look at, and think about, how successful and maximum achievers think, you will see that most—if not all—of them think about the future most of the time. In other words, they think about what they want most of the time. They think about it when they get out of bed. They think about it when they take their shower. They think about it when they eat. They think about it when they are moving from place to place. They are still thinking about it when they are about to go to sleep. If possible, they also want to dream about it in their sleep!

You see, the more you think about your successful future, the more confidence you will have in yourself. The more confidence you have in yourself, the more you like yourself. The more you like yourself, the higher your self-esteem. The higher your self-esteem, the more you radiate your positive energy to the people around you, and the like-minded people around you will get attracted to you from the energy you radiate, and the non-like-minded people will repel you because they don't like the energy that you're radiating.

When you think about your bright future, you will live your life passionately, as you know that your future will be successful, and your way is paved for your success. What can you do to think about your positive future?

Start by thinking what your goal is for the future. Is it to be financially free? Is it to make a specific amount of money? Is it to be fit and healthy most of the time? Is it to be the person that you want to be? Or is it that you never want to work again? Second, describe with clarity what your goal looks like to you. For example, maybe you want to make a million dollars in exactly five years from now. Maybe you want to weigh 50 kilograms by the end of the next year. It's up to you to decide.

Next, describe how your life would be after you've accomplished that goal. Maybe, after you have managed to make a million dollars for yourself, you will know how to make it over and over again, and buy yourself a big home, a beautiful car, and send your kids to get the best education that you can afford. Maybe, after you have managed to weigh 50 kilograms, you will look stunningly beautiful, and you will be able to wear beautiful and expensive clothes; people will talk nicely about your new and beautiful look, and you will be able to attract anyone that you desire.

Here's an exciting exercise for you to do. Imagine that you have a time machine. By using that time machine, you can travel forward to five years from now to see what you have become; you, then, see yourself already achieving the goal that you are thinking right now. Then, you go back to the present time and do everything that you can do to achieve it, because you know that five years from now, you will have achieved it.

Keep Calm

One of the keys for accomplishment and performance is to keep calm. People are one hundred percent emotion. They think with emotion, and they justify it with their intelligence. That's why most people can easily get into an emotional state, whether it is anger, sadness, happiness, or so on.

As Blair Singer said, *"High emotion yields low intelligence."* What this means is, when your emotions are high, it almost fully takes yourself over, which then leaves little to no space for your intelligence.

Just think about when you are angry. You will blurt out anything that you are thinking and feeling. You will do things that might be unacceptable compared to when your intelligence is still high. You will be difficult to control.

However, when you keep yourself calm most of the time, you will be able to think rationally. You will prevent yourself from regretting what you did when you were being highly emotional. You will be able to make the best decisions that will lead you to your success. You will be able to save lots of time and money, and effort and energy, when you make decisions while you're being highly intelligent, compared to when you're being highly emotional.

One of the ways to get yourself out of your emotional state, and get your intelligence up higher again, is to shift your mood from negative to positive. First, you have to identify the mood that you are in. Make sure that you identify it clearly. Ask yourself, "What mood am I currently in?" Ask the question to yourself over and over until you are able to describe your mood with clarity. Possibly, the mood that you're in is one of sadness, anger, depression, or demotivation, but it is only the one that is on the surface. Find your mood that lies beneath the surface, and you will get the clarity on it. By asking the question to yourself over and over again, you will be able to lower your emotions, and increase your intelligence, to be able to think about it more clearly.

Second, think about how you want to feel. This one has to be positive. Instead of feeling sad, angry, or depressed, you may want to feel happy, calm, or cheerful. Ask yourself, "How do I want to feel right now?" Ask this to yourself enough times until you are able think of the one mood that you want to be in.

Third, think about what you can do to make yourself feel the mood that you want to be in. For instance, you may want to feel motivated. So, you can think about the times when you are feeling fully motivated. You can try to feel the feelings that are associated with those times. You can think about what you can, or want to, reward yourself with, if you are able to get yourself to finish what you are doing. Or, maybe, you can just talk about it with someone, or take a few minutes to walk in the park. It only has to be something that can change your mood to positive.

Fourth, choose which method that you want to use from the third step, and start doing it, as soon as possible, to get your mood in a positive state again. At first, you may find this method uncomfortable for you, but, eventually, you will start to understand it and get comfortable using it. I've been using this method since I've known about it, and it has never ceased to amaze me with how I feel afterwards. And this also means that you can do it too.

The Law of Attraction

Perhaps one of the best laws ever discovered in the success arena is the *Law of Attraction*. This law states that you are a living magnet. You attract what you think about most of the time. Your brain has the ability to materialize your thinking, if you think about it long enough, and hard enough, and often enough. This law originally points to the work of the Universe, but I would like to point it to the work of God.

The astonishing fact is: *you see what you believe.* It is very different from what is always said in the community, which is *seeing is believing*. Your mind is very powerful; you are where you are, and are what you are, because of your personal thinking habits. That's why, if you change your mindset, you change your life, as you actually become a different person because of that, and, as a result, you get different outcomes.

I once read a story about two shoe salespeople, named Harry and Larry, who came from two different companies. Both of them were

Be the Best Student

sent to the same country in the African continent, and they were tasked to explore the potential to market shoes in the country. Harry hated the task, and he desired that he would not have to go. But, Larry liked the task; he saw it as a big chance for a new market so that his company could get more sales.

When they both arrived in the specified country, they went to the local market to look for the potential in which to market their company's shoes. Then, they both called back to their offices. Harry, who wished he didn't have to be there, said, "The trip was a money and time waster. There is no potential market for shoes in this country. No one even wears shoes."

Larry, who saw this as a big chance for his company and believed that he could get something out of it, said, "Great trip. This will be our chance to expand our market. Nobody wears shoes."

You become what you think about most of the time. The more you think about what you want to be, the more your mind will radiate its energy to attract whatever you are thinking. Those who keep thinking and talking about what it is that they want, appear to attract more of this into their lives. People who talk and think about negative things, such as what they are angry and upset about, or what they fear and are worried about, also attract those very things into their lives; and they wonder why those things keep coming to them, although they don't want them.

One of the laws that seems related to this law is the *Law of Magnetism*. This law states that the more money you have, the more it will come to you. We live in a world of abundance where money is always more than enough for everyone. When you have lots of money, you will think about all the money that you have, and because you think about it almost all the time, your mind attracts it to you. When you ask for something from God (or the Universe as some people think of it as), He will help you to get what you want when you ask for it consistently enough, often enough, and hard enough, and He will give it to you at the moment which is right for you.

Change Problem into Opportunity

The good news is that we are now living in a world of unlimited possibilities. More possibilities are available today than ever before in history, but the possibilities are different than before. We are now entering the *Golden Age* that people have been dreaming about throughout history. Your job is to take full advantage of it so that you can design your own future. To quote Orpheus Choy, *"Opportunities are right in front of you, but you are the only one deciding whether to grasp them or not."*

Even with all of those possibilities, coming down to us like raindrops in a torrential rain, problems are always there, and they are inevitable, whether we like it or not. Problems are one of the gifts of life, and, sooner or later, we will still have to face them. So, why don't we treat them in a slightly different way?

Most people think of problems as setbacks that are negative, but don't let them affect you—you, the designer of your own future. Optimistic people use their problems to their advantage. They switch their thinking about it from, "Oh, not again!" to "Yes, more opportunities!" They know that they can learn a lot from solving or not solving their problems. They are grateful for all the problems that they have.

When God wants to give you a present, He will give it to you in the form of setbacks. The bigger the setbacks, the more valuable the present is. The bigger the setbacks, the bigger the lesson behind it. The bigger the lesson behind it, the more you can get out of it. The more you can get out of it, the better your life will be, and the wiser you will become.

Be the Best Student

For optimistic people, instead of complaining, they change setbacks into requests. In fact, for every complaint, there are actually requests behind it. Here's an example: Let's say, you are going to have dinner in a beautiful and luxurious restaurant as your way of rewarding yourself for all of the hard work that you've done for the month. When you arrive at the restaurant, the waiter brings you to the table that they've reserved for you. When you arrive at your table, everything seems good for the moment. Later, a group of loud and noisy people arrive, and their table is assigned near your table. Because you don't like noises when you are having your dinner, you call the waiter to complain that the group of people near your table is noisy. And the waiter then asks, "Would you like to change your table to a much quieter place?" You answer, almost immediately, "Sure."

Did you get what the waiter did? He shifts the customer's complaint to a request instead. If you dwell on your problem, you will get more of it. Instead, if you think about what you want, you will also get more of it. Either way, you still have to think about it. Why don't you think of it in a positive way so that you will get positive results?

When you change your focus, you will change your outcome. I once heard a story about a bee and its mission. The mission of the bee was to get honey from all of the flowers that it could, and deliver it back to its nest. That was the obvious thing that was happening. The thing that was happening in the background was that the bee was actually pollinating the flowers without the bee itself realizing it. If the bee could shift its mission to pollinating the flowers instead, it would be able to get to more flowers, and, as a result, it would be able to deliver more honey back to its nest. From this story, you can understand that by changing your mission, or focus, you will change your result or outcome.

Kharisma Khalid

My Final Year Project Story

When I started my Final Year Project, in the third semester of my college years, I received almost no info on how to build it, yet alone how to build its foundation. Thus, I had to read books and articles, and learn by trial-and-error, just to find out how I could build its foundation.

I did the research from eight o'clock in the morning until ten o'clock in the evening, every day, for seven consecutive days. I read quite a number of books, articles, and guides related to my project. I watched quite a number of videos on how I could understand the backbone of it, and also did a lot of work by trial-and-error on the subjects related to my project in order to find out which method worked.

By the end of the seventh day, I had almost no outcome on how to build my project's foundation. I almost gave up because I didn't have, and couldn't find, any project to model it from. I also didn't think that it was possible for me to build it, using the platform that I was using, because I couldn't find any successful project related to it on the Internet or at the library. Even so, I said to myself, "Let's do it for at least seven more days. I am currently in the research and development process, so I can't expect it to get results in just a few days." So, I continued with it for seven more days.

Up to the thirteenth day, I almost gave up, because all of the trial-and-error I had done so far came to no avail. I had read hundreds of articles, how-to guides, books, posts, and project documentations that were related to my project since the day I started working on it, but I still got no results. I even, almost, wanted to change the project I was working on.

By almost midnight on the fourteenth day, after tens of thousands of minutes spent on research and development, and after hundreds of dollars spent on buying, subscribing, and purchasing the materials, services, and resources needed for building the foundation of my project, and after hundreds of thoughts and feelings being shifted, for the very first time, I managed to build a working foundation for my project. I was so extremely happy at that time that I celebrated like crazy; I managed to build my project's foundation after all of the things I had spent to get it.

Thomas Edison, the inventor of the light bulb, and the founder of the General Electric Company, once said, *"I have not failed. I've just found 10,000 ways that won't work."* Imagine what would have happened if Thomas Edison had stopped doing his research and development in building a working light bulb. Chances are, we would still be using oil lamps or candles to light our houses. Chances are, the greater invention and engineering in lighting would not be available today. Chances are, we would never get to see the beautiful lights that light up the capital cities of the world during the night.

Whether we realize it or not, being optimistic has its own reward. When you become optimistic, you will be confident about what you can do; you will think better about your limitless future; you will keep calm most of the time, knowing that high emotion yields low intelligence; you will think about what you want all the time because you know that you will attract it into your life; you will convert your problems into opportunities; and you will make requests instead of complaining, because you know that you are an optimistic person.

STEP 5: PRACTICE SELF-CONFIDENCE

What is Self-Confidence?

Self-confidence is the act of trusting yourself with your own ability, action, and decision. Self-confidence is more about *positive knowing* rather than *positive thinking*. Self-confidence is something that you will have when you know that you have done something that is true to yourself, and you trust yourself that you will get the best possible result out of it. Self-confidence is all about having confidence in yourself.

Positive knowing is about you knowing more about yourself, your actions, your decisions, your judgments, your intelligences, and your abilities to do something while staying true to yourself. When you stay true to yourself, your self-confidence will come naturally to you, as though you already have had it for a long time, because you actually already have it, and you only need to bring it out in the open. There are tons to gain by being real and true to yourself. Even the World's #1 Wealth Coach, JT Foxx, said, *"I'd rather be hated for being real, than be loved for someone I am not."*

Positive thinking is way different from positive knowing. Positive thinking is about being optimistic. Positive thinking is about you expecting the best out of everything, whether you do anything in your power to achieve it or not. Even if you don't take action to achieve something that you want, you can still have that positive thinking, but not positive knowing. Positive knowing is only acquired when you have done everything that you can to achieve something that you want, and because of the series of actions that you took, you know positively that the outcome of what you have done is positive.

Kharisma Khalid

When you have self-confidence, you will be able to stay true to yourself. When you have self-confidence, you will talk with power, present with energy, and walk with pride. When you have self-confidence, you will be able to get the best out of everything that you do. When you have self-confidence, your hidden abilities will unleash themselves to aid you for your accomplishment and performance. When you have self-confidence, your life will never be the same again.

It is said that it is very rare for people with self-confidence to be remembered for it. I've been to a lot of seminars, and I've met and greeted thousands of people since the first time I went to one. I have had many people say things like this to me at almost every seminar that I have gone to: *"Since the first time I saw you in this seminar, I've recognized that you are very different from everyone else here. It is like you have some kind of energy radiating out from yourself."*

One of the things that you can do to have self-confidence is to learn more to know more. The more you learn, the more you know, and the more self-confidence you will have. Another thing that you can do is for you to have better understanding about something. If you know that two times five equals ten, will you have confidence in your answer then? That is also a part of self-confidence. Besides that, you can also do everything in your power in order to get a specific result. If you want to pass your exam with flying colors, you will have the self-confidence in your result when you have done everything that you can to get it.

When I was in my college years, every time I had exams, I did everything that I could to obtain the results that I wanted. Therefore, every time I got my results, they were always the best that I could have done during that time, and I never regretted any of them.

Be the Best Student

The Man Who Met John D. Rockefeller

I've listened to and read a story about a man who was in severe trouble in his business. He'd lost a number of big contracts and sales. He was still in debt for hundreds of thousands of dollars. His suppliers and creditors were chasing him for their money, even though their due dates were still far off. He was very depressed during that time. He didn't know whether he should continue to persevere to get his business back on its feet again, or just announce bankruptcy and let his shop close. So, he decided to go for a walk in a park near his house that evening to think about it completely and to decide what to do.

In the park, he was standing on a small bridge looking down into the water when an old man suddenly appeared out of the bush nearby. Seeing how gloomy the man's look was, the old man stopped and stood next to the man who was still standing on the bridge. The old man asked the man, "What happened?"

Somehow, the man told the old man about his business issues and how his business was now on the verge of bankruptcy, although he still thought that the business was a good one and had a bright potential for the future. The old man listened attentively, and then he said, "I think I can help you with your business issues."

The old man pulled out a checkbook from his shirt pocket. He asked the man for his full name, and wrote a check for him. Then, the old man gave the man the check that he wrote. The old man then said, "Take this money. Meet me on this small bridge in exactly three hundred and sixty-five days from today, and you can pay me back then." The old man then went back into the bush from where he had appeared from, and, by the time the man realized, he was gone.

The man then looked at the check and realized that it had been written by John D. Rockefeller, and it was for five hundred thousand dollars. Initially, the man thought he would use the money from the check to solve his business issues. But, then, he decided to hold on to that check first, knowing that he could use it at any time. With refreshed passion, he went back and did whatever he could to revive his business. In just nine months, his business was thriving, was debtless, and making more money than ever.

Exactly three hundred and sixty-five days later, the man went back to stand on the bridge in the park to meet the old man, to give him his uncashed check back and to tell him his amazing story. At the fixed time, the old man appeared from out of the bush nearby, once more. When the man was about to tell the old man his exciting story and give him his check back, a nurse suddenly came out of the bush from where the old man had come from and grabbed the old man's arm. The nurse apologized to the man and explained that the old man always escaped from his care home nearby, and went around this park telling people that he was John D. Rockefeller. The nurse then took the old man away.

The man was speechless, but he suddenly realized that everything that he had accomplished so far was based on his beliefs and his confidence in himself, despite the fact that the information that lead him to it was actually made-up. It was his own self-confidence that unleashed his inner potential and brought him to his own success.

Effects of Self-Confidence

Self-confidence is one of the keys to success. A lot of successes have been built on the foundation of self-confidence. Just think about the Wright Brothers. If they had thought that they could not build a flying machine, they would never have been able to build it, and we may never have been able to travel by flying. J.M. Barrie, the writer of the story, Peter Pan, once said, *"The moment you doubt whether you can fly, you cease forever to be able to do it."* Because the Wright Brothers had the confidence in what they could do, they didn't care about what other people said about their idea, and hence, they were able to build their first aircraft together.

By having self-confidence, you will increase your self-esteem. Self-esteem is the feeling of liking yourself. Self-esteem is about feeling that you are a worthy person. Self-esteem is about thinking that you are valuable. Self-esteem and self-confidence go hand-in-hand with each other. The more you like yourself, the higher your self-confidence. The higher your self-confidence, the more valuable you think you are.

People with self-confidence are downright sexy. You can figure this out yourself by looking at a person around you who you think has self-confidence. Even if you initially think that they are not that attractive, when you see that they have self-confidence in whatever they do, your opinion of them will change forever.

One of the people that can be an example that you can look at is Nick Vujicic. Nick Vujicic is an inspirational and motivational keynote speaker. He is the founder of the company, Attitude is Altitude. He is the author of the New York Times bestselling book, *Unstoppable*. The shocking thing about him is that he has no limbs—no feet and no hands. But, when you see him talk on the stage or video, you will be amazed by how confident is he. He has a lot of money and he has inspired tens of thousands of people around the world.

Lizzie Velásquez was considered to be *the world's ugliest woman* because she was born with a very rare disease that prevents her body from accumulating fat, which is essential for building people's looks. She was bullied throughout her childhood because of her looks. Because of her condition during that time, she was inspired to speak out against bullying. She became a motivational speaker. She had so much confidence in herself that she was determined to do so. I haven't been to any of her talks or seminars yet, but one of my friends had the opportunity to do so. When he got back from her talk, he said that Lizzie was one of prettiest women he had ever seen in his entire life. Why? Because she had confidence in herself.

Lao Tzu once said, *"Because one believes in oneself, one doesn't try to convince others. Because one is content with oneself, one doesn't need others' approval. Because one accepts oneself, the whole world accepts him or her."* When a person has self-confidence in themselves, they don't really care about what other people think about them. When you have self-confidence, your hidden abilities will unlock themselves to help you achieve your goals, just like what happened to Nick Vujicic and Lizzie Velásquez. Because they have self-confidence, they stay true to themselves, and they know clearly what they want to achieve in their lives. It has opened them up to unlimited possibilities, and you can have this too.

Act-As-If Practice

Imagine the moment when you have made your very first million dollars. You are now officially a millionaire. How do you feel? As you scan the statement of your bank account, the total balance in it is more than six digits. You feel amazing. You think of all you have done so far to get those numbers in your bank account. You think of your sweat and tears from all of the hard work you've done so far.

Now, you are worth one million dollars and more; how will you think of yourself? Do you think that you can accomplish anything as long as you put your mind to it? Do you think that you are worth more than you can ever think of? Do you think that you have more confidence in yourself than ever before?

Now that you have a lot of money, what will you do differently from now on? How will you do things differently from now on? How will you look at your world differently from now on? How will you look at the people around you differently from now on? How will you act differently from now on? How will you talk differently from now on?

Now that you have already made your very own one million dollars, how will you manage your finances differently? What subject are you going to learn more of? Who are you going to be friends with? Who are you going to network with? Where will you usually hang out at?

Commit today to take actions for your goal as though you have already achieved it. When you act as though you have already accomplished your goal, your subconscious mind will think that you have really achieved it, and it will activate the *Law of Attraction* by sending the message to God (or the Universe) that you have already accomplished your goal, and He will reply to you by giving you things that are related to you accomplishing your goal.

For example, when you are already a millionaire, you will feel great. You will think of yourself as great. You will think that you can accomplish anything as long as you put your mind to it. You will think that you are worthy. You will have a tremendous amount of self-confidence. You will only spend your time doing things that contribute to you making more money. To cite Orpheus Choy, *"Time is evenly given to every human in this world. If you feel you are not up to your deserved net worth yet, rethink how to make the full use of each of your minute to achieve that!"*

You will look at the world as though you can see opportunities to make money from everywhere. You will look at the people close to you, dearly and happily. You will act as though you will always succeed. You will talk with power. You will manage your finances carefully.

You will learn more of what you like. You will be friends only with those who will, and can, contribute to your success, accomplishment, and performance. You will be networking with the best people available in the community, or in the world, and you will always hang out at the places where those people usually hang out.

Did you notice, if you do all of the things that you say you would do after you've accomplished your goal, before you even achieve it, you may be able to accomplish that goal of yours faster? You have the ability to develop in yourself an outstanding set of values by acting as though you already have them. The more you practice those values, the faster they will become permanently instilled in you. As Dr. Robert Anthony said, *"Act as if you have already achieved your goal and it is yours."*

Kill Fear or Fear Kills

My wonderful teacher and trainer in creating an online business empire, Larry Loik, always said this to his students: *"Kill fear or fear kills."* Fear is, and will always be, the utmost enemy of mankind. Fear is what holds us back from taking action on something. The feeling of fear comes from the reptilian cortex of our brain, and it is what helps us survive.

Fear is absolutely needed for our survival. It helps us to think before we cross the road. It helps us to stay away from danger. It helps us to analyze the situation for danger. It helps us to stay alert most of the time. It helps us to be prepared in case of emergency. It helps us in our *fight-or-flight* decisions. We should be grateful for our fear, as, because of it, we are still alive.

What is meant right here, though, is that excessive fear is never good. It sabotages us from getting the success that we want. It holds us back from reaching our goals. It keeps us from doing something new. It makes us stay comfortable at where we are, and that sure is bad.

Be the Best Student

For instance, when you are doing something new, you may feel and think that it will not work, and because you think so, it usually will not work. Remember the *Law of Attraction*? But, nothing works the first time. After the first time you do something, and it is not working, guess what? Your fear kicks in, and it says that it will never work for you, thus you stop doing it altogether. Can you relate to this?

Another example: When you do something that is not considered as common in your community, such as speaking or acting on the stage, you may be afraid of what others will think of you. Maybe you will tell yourself something along these lines: "What if they say bad things about me behind my back? What if they don't like what I do? What if they won't support me for my actions?" If you do something that you consider as being positive and good and true to yourself, it will seldom turn out to be bad. Because of this kind of fear and self-talk, you are possibly sabotaging yourself from doing something to achieve your goal.

If you are to face fear in any situation, here is what you can do to work around it. I initially heard this from the British wealth coach, Kevin Green, but I got to learn this from my trainer, Blair Singer. First, remember any success that you've had so far. Remember how you felt about it. Second, make a fist, pull it in, and energetically say, "Yes!" This anchors the feeling related to your success so that you can feel more of it by adding action into it. Do it several times until you can feel the confidence from your previous success experience. Every time, when you feel afraid of taking action on something, do this to increase your confidence and energy. Third, do the thing that you feared. Commit to finish it. Commit to do it till it ends.

When you are able to control your fear, you will become unstoppable. You will be able to achieve your dreams faster than most people. Your self-confidence will rise through the roof. You will love and value yourself more than ever. FEAR is False Evidence Appearing

Real. As Nelson Mandela said, *"The brave man is not he who does not feel afraid, but he who conquers that fear."*

Goal Setting

A goal is an achievement that you want to accomplish. A goal is a point where you want to be or something you want to have in the future. A goal is an ambition. A goal is a specific aim. A goal is also an anticipated result. Even will all of those being written, not everyone has a goal. Only those who know what they want in their life have it.

Great people are those who definitely know that they were born in this world to accomplish something extraordinary with their lives. They have a future vision of having and getting something better than their current situation. They are the leaders of their own lives. Because they realize that no one is going to lead them to achieve their goals, they commit to lead their own lives no matter what it takes.

But in order to be great, you must have a clear sense of direction, or goal. When you have a clear goal, you know exactly where you want to be and what you want to have in the future. When you have a clear goal, you will be able to stretch yourself out of your own self-limiting boundaries. When you have a clear goal, you will be able to draw out the very best from within yourself.

To create a clear goal, you must fulfil these five rules. I've learned about this from a management class that I attended during my college years. I call it The SMART Rule.

The first rule is: Specific. Your goal must be as specific as possible, leaving no details behind.

The second rule is: Measurable. Your goal must be measurable. If you can't measure it, you will not be motivated to accomplish it, as you will not know whether you've accomplished it or not.

The third rule is: Achievable. Your goal must be achievable. You will never achieve something that you can't do in the first place.

The fourth rule is: Realistic. Your goal must be realistic so that you will feel that you can achieve it.

The fifth rule is: Time bound. When your goal is time bound, you know exactly when you want your goal to be achieved. Orpheus Choy once said, *"Be visionary to accomplish your dreams through massive actions within specific deadlines."* One more thing: Make sure that your goal also follows the 3P Rule—Personal, Present, and Positive.

Here's an example that you can follow: You weigh sixty kilograms, so, your goal may be: I will weigh fifty kilograms by 11:59 p.m., Pacific Standard Time, on 31st December 2017. Questions that you have to ask regarding it: Is it specific? Yes, as it is not arguable. Is it measurable? Yes, because I wrote that I want to weigh fifty kilograms. Is it achievable? Yes, because now I weigh sixty kilograms, and I just need to shed ten kilograms. Is it realistic? Yes, because I know that I am able to do so. Is it time bound? Yes, because I put the time, 11:59 p.m., and the date, 31st December 2017, and I even put the time zone, Pacific Standard Time, to make sure it is very specific and not arguable. One more question: Is that goal of mine personal, present, and positive?

Here's an exercise that you can do to practice your creation of clear goal setting. Write down ten goals that you want to accomplish within a year, using the SMART and the 3P Rule, on a piece of paper. This very action of writing your goal is called psycho neuro motor activity, which means that it activates your three primary senses, which will help you to program your subconscious mind to activate the *Law of Attraction*, to aid you in getting what you want. By the end of this year, or next year, you will be amazed by how many goals from the list that you've accomplished earlier than for what your goal had been time bound. Also, I've created a template for you to create your goal by using the SMART and 3P Rules. Just fill in the blanks, and your goal is done! Check it out at www.TheBestStudentBook.com via *Goal Setting Template* bonus.

STEP 6: OUTPERFORM YOUR COMPETITORS

Competitors Are Inevitable

In business and in life, competitors are unavoidable. Whether we want it or not, whether we realize it or not, they are always there for us. In business, you can think of your competitors as the ones who may have the same target market as yours, or the ones who may sell the same product as yours. In life, you can think of your competitors as the ones who may want the same job as you do when job hunting, or the ones who may want to get the same woman as you want for their relationship.

Because we cannot escape from the fact that we will always have a competitor, and because we cannot change facts, instead of thinking of it in a negative way, whining about it, or complaining about it, let's think of it in a positive and optimistic way that will be beneficial for us.

Take advantage of it to reflect upon yourself. You can actually see yourself from the reflection of your competitors. In business, maybe your competitors have more customers than you. What can you see in yourself from it? Probably, you can see that your business is not doing enough to create and keep a customer. Think positively of the reflection that you can see from your competitors, because if you do it negatively, it won't do you any good.

Besides that, competitors are what drives you to keep getting better over time. Your competitors are also like you—they always want to outperform you so that they can be the best. They will always find ways to outperform you. They keep our brain thinking about what we can do to outperform them. Thus, take advantage of it by getting one step ahead of them every time they get one step ahead of you. Nancy Lopez, the American professional golfer, once said, *"A competitor will find a way to win. Competitors take bad breaks and use them to drive themselves just that much harder. Quitters take bad breaks and use them as reasons to give up. It's all a matter of pride."*

Furthermore, competitors are the source of your greatness. As Herbert Hoover said, *"Competition is not the only basis of protection to the consumer, but is the incentive to progress."* You can shine better when you have competitors rather than not; you can become number one, and be the best, because of your competitors; you can do better when you have competitors; you can know much more about yourself when you have competitors; you can learn much more when you have competitors; and this list is still far from its end.

Moreover, competitors teach us about what we don't know. Just take a look at Kodak's film camera: Just more than a decade ago, their business was thriving. In just a few short years, by the time they knew it, their business was on the verge of bankruptcy; it was turned around by their competitors who introduced digital cameras and understood that they would be in the photo sharing business. Because they didn't learn how their photo-related business was evolving, they lost their billion dollar market share.

Take advantage of your competitors. Learn from them. Use them to shine more brightly. When you take advantage of your competitors, you will be able to improve more in a few short months than most people do in a few long years.

You Are Your Own Business

Do you realize what it means when people say, "Mind your own business?" The fact is, you are a business entity, managed by yourself, for yourself. Everything about business can be related to yourself—marketing, financing, asset management, leadership, customer service, human training, etc.

Let's read an example here: You are in charge of your own financing. How you acquire and manage your money is up to you. Maybe you work at a job or do business to earn your money. And then, maybe you use your money to pay your bills or to make more money, or to go on vacations. No one but yourself is going to acquire and manage your money for you.

One more example here: human training. You are in charge of your own learning and training. The more you learn, the more money you will possibly make. When you stop learning, your earning ability will decrease from time to time, and by the time you know it, you are struggling just to get by. No one but yourself is going to manage what you learn. You are the one who chooses what and when you want to learn it.

Did you see how you can relate business to yourself? When you realize that you are your own business, you will realize that you have more potential than you ever had before; you will be able to look at yourself objectively; you will be able to measure your performance; you will be able to learn more about yourself in a few months than most people do in a few years; and you will be able to outperform your competitors faster than you think.

In order to think that you are a business entity, start by thinking of yourself objectively. This means that you think of yourself from the outside. Step outside of yourself; look at yourself as though you are looking at yourself from the view of other people. Then, list the managements available in a business and ask questions about yourself related to those managements; for instance, leadership management, or the head office of your business. Here are some questions that you can ask yourself objectively: Are you leading your own life? Are you the one who is making progress? Are you in charge of all departments available within yourself? How well are you managing them?

In regard to customer service management, or how you treat the people around you, here are some questions that you can ask yourself objectively: How well did you treat the people around you? Did you treat them the way you would want to be treated yourself? How are your social skills with the people around you? How well is your communication with them?

Your competition is also a part of your business, and it falls under your strategic planning department. This department is in charge of strategic planning. When you want to outperform your competitors, you do need strategic plans to do so. You need to have at least one strategic plan to outperform your competitors, because as Alex Mandossian said, *"Version one is better than version none."* And one of the plans that you can use to outperform your competitors will be revealed in the upcoming pages. To get more clarity on what you can do to get to where you want to be in the future from your current situation, I suggest you do Gap Analysis. Check it out at www.TheBestStudentBook.com, via *Gap Analysis Report* bonus to see if it can help you.

Winners Focus On Winning

When it comes to outperforming competitors, most people can't help thinking about their competitors every time; they will always think about what they can do to outperform them; they will always think that they have to bring their enemy down; and they will always find ways to do whatever they can to get ahead of their enemies, by every means possible.

But, as for the winners, they only focus on winning, and are their own greatest enemy. For the high achievers, they do whatever they can to be the best. For the high performers, they always aim to be at the top, and always aim to beat their own records in their competition because they know, from the very beginning, that they can always do better.

For the losers, they focus on winners. They think about what they can do to outperform their competitors, even by just a bit. They always think about outperforming their competitors, but not about being the best. They are always leapfrogging their competitors, and, as a result, their position will also always change from time to time; they need to know their competitors' advances before they can advance themselves.

When you focus on winning, you still think about your competitors as your source of learning. Otto von Bismarck once said, *"The wise man learns from the mistakes of others."* When you learn from the mistakes of others, you will save thousands of dollars, and minutes, or even hours, than if you had made the mistake yourself and had to find the solution for it. When you learn from your competitors, your competitors will be the ones who do the research for you while you observe them and learn from them, and you can make your plan to be the best based on your competitors' courses of action that you've studied.

Winners stay true to themselves in order to win. They compete using their very own style. They have their very own set of values to be followed in their course of actions. They know exactly who they want to be if they were to pursue it. They have their own way to do anything they want to do. They are very unique themselves, because they know that, when they follow someone, they will be the *someone* that they are following.

Edward de Bono once said, *"Companies that solely focus on competition will die. Those that focus on value creation will thrive."* What can you do to focus on value creation to win? What can you do to focus on increasing your own value in order for you to thrive in this fast-paced world?

First, find out what you want to be or what you want to win in. If you don't know where you want to go, any road will get you to anywhere. Perhaps you want to be someone who has the best results in your field. Perhaps you want to make a specific amount of money in order to prove to yourself that you can do it. Second, figure out why you want to be it or why you want to win in it. The more answers you have for this step, the more motivated you will be in wanting to achieve it. Maybe you want to make that specific amount of money so that you will know how to make it over and over again. Third, discover how you can be it or how you can win it. Think of what you can do to reach your identified destination. Maybe you have to learn a specific subject to gain it.

Identify Your Competitors

One of the most important questions in identifying your competitors is: Who exactly are your competitors? Your ability to answer this question correct to its fact will determine your success in winning your competition. When you gather information about your competitors, make sure that it is correct and unarguable so that you can make the best decision based on the accurate data that you've gathered.

Learn everything that you can about your competitors. Leave no space for doubts or questions when you gather your competitors' data. Get the data on their target markets. Know about their current technologies and advances. Recognize their suppliers and creditors and who works for and with them. The more data you gather on your competitors, the more you will learn about them, and from them, and the better the quality of the decision and plan that you will make from those data.

Be the Best Student

One of the most common mistakes people make when competing with other people or businesses is that they tend to underestimate their competitors. When they underestimate their competitors, they will start to take their competitors easily, they will start to take their competition easily, and that will be the moment where their competitors learn about what they think, and plan and take actions to outperform them.

The rule for identifying, thinking about, and understanding your competitors is: Never underestimate your competitors. Your competitors absolutely know something that you do not know; your competitors definitely have their own plans and ways to outperform you; your competitors may know what you are thinking right now, and what you will do afterwards; and your competitors may also have done their research on you or your business without you being aware of it.

The other mistake that most people commonly make in identifying and understanding their competitors is thinking that their competitors are only around and near them. In this twenty first century, with the rapid growth of the Internet and communication methods, either in business or in life, our competitors can be from anywhere in the world. For example, individuals from Australia may be able to sell their products in America. Before the availability of the Internet, this was next to impossible, unless they were in the import and export business. After the Internet came along, this became extremely possible, and more and more individuals sell internationally now than ever counted in human history.

The other rule for identifying, thinking about, and understanding your competitors is: Your competitors can be from anywhere. If you are able to get to know quite a number of them, you will be able to gather a tremendous amount of data related to your competitors, and you will be able to learn more and more about them, which you can use to improve yourself.

Only talk positively about your competitors. Think of them as someone whom you respect, because, the fact is, you should respect them, because they know something that you don't, and they have the ability to outperform you. When you talk positively about your competitors, your prospects and customers will respect you because of that, as not everyone is able to do so because of their own negativity.

Clarify Your Purpose of Competition

Why do you want to compete with your competitors in the first place? Isn't it enough just to live your life, or just to survive in your business just as it is, so that you can just live for another day? If yes, what is the thrill in living your life like that? Great men and women understand the fact that they are born in this world with a mission. They understand that whatever they do in this world is to fulfil their mission. They understand that they outperform their competitors because they want to achieve their mission. Even a bee has a mission in their life, even though they may not know about it, which is to pollinate the flowers that it visits.

Why do you want to compete with your competitors? You must have reasons for it, so that you can know how to do it. Maybe you want to outperform your competitors because you want to be the best. Ovid, the Roman poet, said, *"A horse never runs so fast as when he has other horses to catch up and outpace."* You may want to outperform your competitors because you want to learn from them. As Malcolm X wrote, *"Any time you find someone more successful than you are, especially when you're both engaged in the same business, you know they're doing something that you aren't."*

Possibly, you want to outperform your competitors because you want to enjoy the journey of it. To quote Shannon L. Alder, *"I am convinced that the jealous, the angry, the bitter and the egotistical are the first to race to the top of mountains. A confident person enjoys the journey, the people they meet along the way and sees life not as a competition. They reach the summit last because they know God isn't at the top waiting for them. He is down below helping his followers to understand that the view is glorious where ever you stand."*

Whatever reasons you want to have for your purpose of competition, make sure you understand it clearly, and you make it so easy to understand that even a five-year-old child would know and understand what it is, if you were to tell them. This is important so that you will not doubt it's meaning later, and so that you can re-evaluate your purpose of competition from time to time so it matches your own set of values.

Whatever your purpose for competition is, if it is positive and true to yourself, go for it. Don't be caring much about what other people will think of you because of it. I heard a quote from one of my trainers during my college years, *"There will always be someone who will hate you because of anything,"* and I got the full quote from Shannon L. Alder, *"They will hate you if you are beautiful. They will hate you if you are successful. They will hate you if you are right. They will hate you if you are popular. They will hate you when you get attention. They will hate you when people in their life like you. They will hate you if you worship a different version of their God. They will hate you if you are spiritual. They will hate you if you have courage. They will hate you if you have an opinion. They will hate you when people support you. They will hate you when they see you happy. Heck, they will hate you while they post prayers and religious quotes on Pinterest and Facebook. They just hate. However, remember this: They hate you because you represent something they feel they don't have. It really isn't about you. It is about the hatred they have for themselves. So smile today because there is something you are doing right that has a lot of people thinking about you."*

Plan Ahead

Plan ahead on how you can outperform your competitor. Make it as your goal until you've reached it. Abraham Lincoln said, *"Give me six hours to chop down a tree and I will spend the first four sharpening the axe."* When you plan ahead, you can reach your goals faster than most people; you can stay on your course of action; you can measure your progress and success; and you can identify what worked and what didn't. When you plan ahead, you can plan better next time. The more you plan, the more you can plan. So, plan ahead so that you can reach your goal faster and stay focused on reaching it.

What can you do to plan ahead to outperform your competitors? First, know what you want to accomplish. What is it that you want to accomplish by outperforming your competitors? This question is made based on the previous subchapter. Your answers to this question may be to shine brighter yourself, or to be the best in your field, or to take advantage of your competitors' knowledge, or whatever it is that you want, as long as it is positive and is true to your values. Yogi Berra said, *"If you don't know where you are going, you'll end up someplace else."*

Second, think about the things that you can do to accomplish it. List them on paper and sort them based on their sequence or priority, whichever suits you the best.

Third, predict your competitor's course of actions or reactions. If you do *something*, then what will your competitor do to react to your *something*?

Fourth, make a number of plans based on your predictions. There might be three or four or five, or even more reactions based on every action that you put in your plan. For every action of your competitor that you've predicted, make sure that you reply to it with the action that suits you. This might be exhausting to do, but the success of your mission or goal will depend on the plans that you've created and evaluated. Nowadays, there are lots of software that you can use to create plans like this, so you don't need to rewrite the same thing over and over again.

Fifth, run the plan, and follow along your competitor's course of actions and reactions. Run through your plan based on your competitor's responses. In this step, you will also need to identify what worked and what didn't, so that the next time you do it, you will know what you want to avoid putting in your plans.

Sixth, continue to add and improve your plan over time. Your competitors may change their thinking, plans, and course of actions over time. Your job is to improve your plans earlier, before you recognize that they have changed their plans, so that you can stay ahead of them. I've watched and read a number of story lines related to special planning, and it never ceases to amaze me how thorough they made their plan, and that their opponents follow their plans exactly as they want. If they can do it, you definitely can do it.

By the end of this chapter, you should know that competitors are inevitable. You are in charge of your own corporation. Winners focus on winning most of the time. Identifying your competitors is necessary before you can outperform them. When you clarify your purpose of competition, make it as clear as possible—and plan ahead to stay focused on your goals.

STEP 7: BE A LIFELONG STUDENT

Read Books and Listen to Audio Programs

There have never been more books and information than there are today, except for tomorrow—and the days and weeks and months and years ahead. According to recent research done by Dr. Jim Allen and Dr. Rolf van der Velden of Maastricht University, it was discovered that, on average, almost thirty-three percent of the skills acquired in tertiary education were rendered obsolete seven years later. This means that what you've learned and mastered today may be useless in seven years.

Nowadays, there is a trend in the IT industry about the *Internet of Things*, which means that everything can be connected and controlled via the Internet. According to a recent study by IBM, the *Internet of Things* will lead to the doubling of information every twelve hours! According to an article by Cisco, by the end of 2015, the annual global internet traffic will have reached the zettabyte threshold. A zettabyte is equal to 1,000,000,000,000 gigabytes. Wow! That sure is a lot of data, and the *Internet of Things* is already trending, which also means that the amount of information available today is already so much!

Take advantage of the amount of information available today to increase your worth and knowledge. The more you learn, the more you can learn, and the more you can earn, the more you will be worth. No one is worthier than someone who always increases their worth themselves. As Oscar Wilde said, *"It is what you read when you don't have to that determines what you will be when you can't help it."*

Kharisma Khalid

Books are the food for the mind. When you read books—I mean, non-fiction books—you will be able to fill your mind with knowledge and wisdom. You will be able to know more than you knew before. You will have more confidence than you had before. Your thinking process will be better than that of most people who do not read books.

Maybe you don't have the time to read books all the time, like when you are driving or cycling, or walking, or doing your dishes. We now live in a world where technology helps us to get and do what we want for us. You can now listen to audio books while you are walking or travelling from one place to another, or while doing other things. If the average person takes thirty minutes to go to work every day, and he or she takes another thirty minutes to go back home, and he or she has to work five days a week, for an average of fifty weeks per year, that translates into two hundred and fifty hours of commuting to and from work every day! If you use all that time during which you are commuting, to listen to audio books, you will be one of the highest paid people in your industry, because you will know more and will be able to do more by using that knowledge, than those who don't!

So, commit today to read books or listen to audio programs for at least one hour every morning when you are getting ready to start your day. If you commit to do so, I suggest that you do the *90-Day Best Student Conditioning Program* that can remind you about it, and that you can get at www.TheBestStudentBook.com. This will boost your mood to get motivated for the day, and if you finish reading a book in a week, it will translate to about fifty books per year and five hundred books in ten years. You will absolutely be making lots of money and will be worth a lot more by then, or, at least, you will be needing a much bigger house in which to store your books.

Be the Best Student

Go to Seminars

I once read a quote which was written along these lines, *"Take all the seminars that you can afford, one of them will change your life."* It is true. Before this, I had never liked the idea of going to seminars because I was not comfortable with it, or its environment.

After the very first seminar I went to (because I wanted very much to go to it), it changed my life dramatically. Since then, I look at myself objectively. I think before I act. I manage my finances carefully. I read more books in a few months than I've read all my life. I listen to audio programs while I am travelling from one place to another, and I increase my self-confidence every time I go to any seminar.

Every time, after I go to any seminar, I always change myself for the better, because, each time, I realize something about myself, I become aware of it, I learn something new, and I meet someone new. I am also able to meet wonderful people from all over the world. And, because of that, I can network with them and learn from their wise insights.

When you go to seminars, you will be able to learn from the people who have read hundreds, or even thousands, of books in their lifetime. You will be able to network with people who have the same mindset and way of thinking as you. You will be able to get to know incredible people. You will realize something about yourself and you will change for the better.

When you go to seminars, you will be able to join the people in the top twenty percent of your community. You may be able to learn something that you can't from the books. You will be able to increase your self-esteem and your self-confidence. You will be in a safe context where you will be able to learn and grow exponentially compared to under normal circumstances.

Commit today to go to at least one seminar on your chosen subject or topic every year. Whether it is on business, self-help, soft skills like public speaking, or mind setting, it is up to you to decide. Your goal in attending seminars is to learn something new, to network with the best and the most likeminded people, and to get in a safe context for you to learn rapidly.

You will be astonished by how fast you can learn in that kind of environment rather than not. You will be shocked by how you are able to meet the best minds of those whom you would otherwise only know from the Internet, the media, or from books. You will be overwhelmed by the fact that you can network with those remarkable people.

All of this will only happen to you if you go to seminars, where you can experience all of the things I've wrote about here. Maybe you feel hesitant about the very idea of going to seminars. I understand you. I feel you. I used to think that seminars would be boring, with only a lot of talk and no action, like those passive seminars that you may have attended during your school years. If it was like that, it sure would be boring.

But I changed my view on seminars during the first time I went to one. I never knew that seminars outside of my school years would be that interesting and engaging. It changed my view of the world ever since. What prevents you from going to seminars?

What Gets You Here is Not Enough to Keep You There

Have you ever made a large amount of money, and are doing good, but by the time you know it, you are struggling just to make a small amount of change? This literally sums up this subchapter. Initially, you may manage to get to where you were before, because you may have only a few competitors in your arena. But, because people see that you are doing so good in your situation, and because

Be the Best Student

maybe you are selling a specific product at that time, they also start to sell the same product as yours because they expect to be doing as well as you.

As a result, more and more competitors become available for you, and, because you didn't realize it earlier, those competitors of yours start to eat away at your customers. Before you know it, they already have most of them. And, you know what? They thank you for not realizing it earlier, and for giving them your customers. I've been in this kind of situation a few times before, and I have learned something about myself each time. One of the things that I've learned about myself, after I have experienced this kind of situation, is related to the *Parkinson's Law*. This law states that your expenses will rise when your earning ability increases.

For example, normally you just earn about two thousand dollars per month. So, you can only afford to buy small cars, rent a small apartment, and eat home cooked foods. But, when you suddenly earn about five or ten thousand dollars per month, when you had only earned about two thousand dollars per month before, you will increase your expenses to meet your earning ability. Thus, you will start to buy more expensive cars, rent a bigger apartment or house, and eat at restaurants—even luxury ones. This happens because of the *Parkinson's Law*. But you can avoid it by managing your expenses carefully and distinguishing between your needs and wants.

When you are able to distinguish between your needs and wants, you will only buy the things that you need, and the money that is left can be saved or invested in the bank, or the mutual fund manager of your choice. And, because of that, you can apply the *Law of Magnetism*, which states that the more money you save, the more money you will attract to yourself.

One more thing that I've learned, after I experienced this situation, is to find every chance possible to learn and grow. When I got to earn so much money, when usually I would only earn a few bucks, I stopped learning and growing. I became comfortable with my situation. I thought that no one would be able to compete with me because I thought that I was already at the top of my industry. I thought that my competitors could never steal my customers away from me because I had established a strong foundation with them. The biggest thing that I thought I should not have done during that time was that I stopped caring about my business.

Because I was able to earn so much money, I became arrogant. My ego became so big that I even stopped learning, growing, and caring about the business that gave me the money in the first place. When I realized it, I thought to myself, what kind of person am I? But I managed to get a hold of my lessons, and move on to be a better me. If you learn from this lesson of mine, you will be able to avoid one of the pitfalls available in business and personal life.

The Comfort Zone

One of the greatest enemies of success, of all time, is the comfort zone. Most people are not able to get out of their comfort zone because, as its name suggests, they are comfortable staying in their comfort zone. Even I was not able to get out of my comfort zone, because I didn't notice it before. And this very same thing happens to most people, and it is because they don't realize that they are living it.

What is a comfort zone? A comfort zone is a zone where you feel comfortable staying. It is like when you move from one place to another, you feel hesitant in leaving your current place because you have grown comfortable with it. You feel hesitant to move to a new place because you are not familiar with it, but, most importantly, you are not comfortable with it. Allow me to add this word at the end, which is "yet."

Be the Best Student

When you are learning something new, are you comfortable with it yet? No, right? Because you don't know how it will go for you, whether it works for you or not, or whether you can master it or not. Of course, nothing will work the first time. Let's think about the first time you learn a new language; a language which is different than the main language that you use for your daily communications.

The first time you learn a new language, you have to learn it bit by bit, step by step, and little by little. But, because it is a new language, you feel uncomfortable with it, you feel hesitant to learn it, and your self-talk may say that the new language will not fit for you, or it will not be suitable for you. But, because you still have to learn it anyway, you ignore your self-talk and feelings, and continue learning it.

Over time, you start to feel comfortable with it. You start to grasp the words and phrases in the language that you're learning. You start to talk using that new language. You start to learn it easier than before. You start to get along with it. And, as time goes by, you master the basics of the language, just like that. Get the idea?

When you stretch yourself out of your comfort zone, you will be able to see something in a new light. You will see, realize, and learn things that you've never seen, realized, and learned before. You will feel wonderful about yourself because you are able to get out of your comfort zone. Your self-confidence will increase because you know you can get out of your comfort zone. And so much more will happen to you, if and only if, you stretch yourself out of your comfort zone.

One of the methods that you can use to get out of the comfort zone is called the *3A method*. The first step in the 3A method is *Awareness*. In order for you to get out of your comfort zone, you must be aware that you are in your comfort zone. Most people are not aware of it, and that's why they stay in their comfort zone all their life. The second step is *Acceptance*. You must accept the fact that you are in your comfort zone. If you are aware that you are in your comfort zone, but you don't accept it for whatever reason, you will not be able to grow yourself out of it. The third step is *Action*. Take action immediately to get out of your comfort zone. The faster you get out of your comfort zone, the faster you will get the result because of that action of yours. You may feel anxious during the first time you take action to get out of your comfort zone, but don't worry; if you can feel it, it means that you are growing. Keep on keeping on, and you will get to see its result as soon as you are comfortable with it.

The Downfall of Nokia

Nokia Corporation is a company based and founded in Finland. Their main business is in telecommunication and information technology. They were announced to be the world's two hundred and seventy-fourth largest company by the Fortune Global 500, in 2013. For those of you who don't know what Fortune Global 500 is, it is a yearly ranking of the top five hundred companies available in the world, and its ranking is measured by the company's yearly revenue.

Nokia was one of the giant companies that once lead the mobile phone and telecommunication market during its glory years. Nokia was the pioneer of the mobile phone market since 1990. Its brand was so well established in the heart of its users that when people talked about mobile phones, they only mentioned the model, without mentioning its brand, because during that time, people knew that it was only Nokia that they would use.

In 1992, Nokia made the world's first Global System for Mobile communication (GSM) mobile phone, which was called Nokia 1011. It could be used for up to ninety minutes of talk time per full charge, and could store up to ninety-nine contact numbers. In 1999, Nokia launched the Nokia 3210 model, which could be used for up to five hours of talk time per full charge. It sold around a hundred and sixty million units, allowing it to be one of the most successful mobile phones in history.

In 2002, Nokia launched a model called Nokia 6650, which was the world's first third generation (3G) mobile phone. It was built with a rear camera and external mobile antenna. In 2003, Nokia 1100 was launched at a low cost, and sold around two hundred and fifty million units, allowing it to be the best selling consumer electronics product in the world.

In 2007, Apple launched their very first generation of iPhone, and made the touch screen feature popular. Nokia then released their very first touch screen phone in 2008, but it was a year later than Apple. In the same year, the very first version of Android was launched, and Nokia's profit declined. In 2009, the mobile phone market was slowly being eaten away by Apple, BlackBerry, Samsung, HTC, and LG, because these companies started to release their own series of mobile phones.

Nokia realized that they were too late in reacting to the market change, when it was slowly taken over by other companies. Nokia did a lot of things to get their market share to rise again, such as partnering with Microsoft to make smartphones with Microsoft operating systems, laying off quite a number of employees, closing its factory in Finland, moving its base to Asia, and much more. But finally, in April 2014, Nokia sold its Devices and Services business to Microsoft.

What can you learn from this story? First, when you hesitate to adapt to the changes that happen around you, you will be swallowed by it. As what happened with Nokia, they took quite a long time to react to Apple's touch screen phone, which resulted in Apple taking most of their customers away. Next, when you stop learning and growing, and you stay comfortable with your current situation, you will not be making any progress, and your competitors, who continue to make progress, will eat away your customers as soon as possible.

No One Is Better Than You

You are the very best person available in the world. No one else is like you. No one else is better than you. And no one will ever be the same as you, throughout history or later in the future. Putting that aside, if you really wish to be the best person that you can ever be in your entire life, I suggest that you do the *90-Day Best Student Conditioning Program* that you can get at www.TheBest StudentBook.com.

You are unique in each of your senses. You have your own way of thinking, and imagination; you have your very own knowledge that no one else knows; you have your very own mission in this world; you have your very own talents; and you have your very own experiences that no one else will ever experience.

What can you learn from this? Because no one is better than you, and there will never be anyone who is better than you, think and act like you are the best person available in this world, because the thing is—you are. When you act like you are the best person that ever existed in this world, you will know that there are things that only you can do best. Your job is to find that very thing that you can be the best at, and commit to do it wholeheartedly and as best as you can.

When you find the thing that you can be best at, and you put your heart into doing it, you will be able to unlock your hidden potential for achievements and performances. You will feel like you were born to do it. You will excel in that chosen field of yours. You will enjoy doing it very much because it is your passion. And you will appreciate yourself because you will be using your best ability that brings the best out in you.

Be the Best Student

Even though no one is better than you, that doesn't mean that you can just stay in your current situation. The *Law of Cause and Effect* says that for every effect, there is a cause behind it. If you keep doing what you are doing, you will get what you always get, and, eventually, you will stop getting what you always get, because of the changes that happen so fast around you. For the very reason that no one is better than you, you should be the best person that you can ever be. By understanding and applying the *Law of Cause and Effect*, you will be able to have success just like the people who are already successful in their lives.

Maybe, if you are a salesperson, you can start to get better by asking the best salespeople available, questions related to success. Some questions that you may ask them are: What did you do that makes you this successful? What kind of books did you read? What kind of seminars did you attend? What is it that you do differently from other people that makes you stand out in this field so much?

Successful people like to share what they know with the world. But most people won't ask them questions related to it. And successful people don't want to share what they know with average people, because they understand earlier on that average people will not understand what they will be talking about. When you ask successful people about their course of actions that made them successful, they will answer you, most of the time, and when you immediately apply what they have told you, you will see your path to success, piece by piece, and, eventually, it will be like a fully assembled jigsaw puzzle.

BONUS STEP: EXPRESS YOUR GRATITUDE

Develop an Attitude of Gratitude

An attitude of gratitude is the habit of always feeling grateful for something. It doesn't even matter whether you already have it or not.

William Arthur Ward once said, *"Feeling gratitude and not expressing it is like wrapping a present and not giving it."* For everything that you do, have, get, or will get in your life, be grateful and express your gratitude for it. There is always a reason for everything that happens to you or to the things or people around you.

I once read about having deals in business. Sometimes, the best deal in business is that you don't do it in the first place. The reasons for it might be: you know that the client or customer is a complainer or is negative; the deal is not a win-win situation; the business is not going to thrive if you were to venture in it; or many other reasons.

Those reasons might come to you from external or internal sources. Wherever, or however, you obtain it, because of those reasons, you might save yourself lots of time, money, and grief compared to if you were to venture in it; and you should be grateful that it is not happening to you, because you understand it from your deduction of it based on your gathered information.

When you are grateful for what you have, you will always get more of it. When you express your gratitude to the person around you, you will look better in their eyes. I've read many books on leadership, and one of the most powerful and influential ways to lead people is by expressing your gratitude to the people that you are leading. A lot of leaders in this world seldom do this, and their followers think that they are not being appreciated for what they do, which may result in them being less motivated in doing their work, and they will do it halfheartedly instead.

If we express our gratitude, it shows that we are focusing on what we want. It means that we are accepting and acknowledging the things that we have. It shows to our God that we like what He gave us.

How can you develop an attitude of gratitude? Start by accepting what you already have in your life: Accept the fact that you are still alive; accept the fact that you know what you already know; accept the fact that you are reading this book right now; accept the fact that you have a roof over your head; accept the fact that you have a job or business; and accept the fact that you have all the money and assets that you have. If you really want to develop an attitude of gratitude, I suggest that you do the *90-Day Best Student Conditioning Program* that will assist you to do so, and that you can get at www.TheBestStudentBook.com. Get ready to transform your life!

A lot of people want to have what you have, but they can't have it because of whatever reasons, and you should be grateful that you have what you already have. As Epicurus said, *"Do not spoil what you have by desiring what you have not; remember that what you now have was once among the things you only hoped for."*

Always Say Thank You

Ralph Waldo Emerson once said, *"Cultivate the habit of being grateful for every good thing that comes to you, and give thanks continuously. And because all things have contributed to your advancement, you should include all things in your gratitude."*

Be the Best Student

Saying *thank you* is easy for some people, but it might be hard for others. The foundation of gratitude is to acknowledge when you get something from someone. When you find that it is hard to say *thank you*, it might be because you don't want to accept the fact that you are getting something from someone.

When you say *thank you* every time you get something from someone, you will shine in the other person's eyes. You will make the other person feel great and valuable. You will make the other person feel motivated to do something for you. You will leave a great impression on them because they seldom get a *thank you*, and because you gave it to them, they will remember you because of it.

In my life and business, I've been lied to and betrayed many times; whether by people close to me, by people whom I have known for a long time, or by people whom I know from my contacts. Because of those lies and betrayals, my immediate response was, "I hate those people!" I kept hating them since then. Can anyone relate to this? But the more I read books and listen to audio programs, and attend seminars, the more I realize that whatever things have already happened to me, they were just a fact. Whatever happened in the past is categorized as a fact, and no one has the ability to change the past.

So, I reflected on myself and whatever had occurred to me before. From the lies and betrayals that I got, instead of hating the people who did so to me, I found the lesson behind it. What I learned was that lies and betrayals came from human nature, and I couldn't change it.

What I could change was my own thinking and reality. Thus, I learned about what I could do to avoid those betrayals and lies from happening to me again. Some of these ways were by making agreements, memorandums of understanding, and by documenting everything that I could from any deals, statements, or promises that I got. And, in the end, I accepted what had happened to me; and within myself, I thanked those who had wronged me, for, because of them, I learned lessons that might save me more resources in the future.

Commit today to say thank you every time you get anything from anyone. Say thank you when anyone helps you with anything. Say thank you to God every day for everything you have. If you commit to yourself to develop the gratitude habit, I suggest that you do the *90-Day Best Student Conditioning Program* that you can get at www.TheBestStudentBook.com, and that may be able to assist you to develop it faster.

Most people take things for granted. Right now, you still have oxygen to breath. Imagine that oxygen being taken away from you. What would happen to you? You may die in just a minute or two because you have no oxygen to be used for the cells in your body to work. When you think about what would happen to you if you were to lose those gifts, you will start to treasure them and be grateful for them, and that is the mark of great people.

Commit to Accept Praises with Thank Yous

A common problem with people nowadays is that they feel it is hard to accept praises from anyone, whether it is from their friends, relatives, parents, or so on. Whenever they get it, they give it back to its giver.

For instance, the first person may say, "Hey, you have a nice shirt." And the second person may reply with, "Yeah, you have a nice pair of pants too." What happens here is that the praises cancel each other because the first person gave the praise, and then the second person gave it back.

We live in a world of duality—there are ups and downs; there are lefts and rights; there are ins and outs; there are rights and wrongs;

Be the Best Student

and there are gives and takes. We have our hands and our feet. For most cases, we need both in order to make use of our full ability. What will happen if you only have a left foot and a right hand? Chances are, you will not be able to balance yourself. The same thing applies to this praise and thank you thing. They also need balance in order for them to work flawlessly.

What will happen if there are only givers but no receivers? Chances are, the givers will not be able to give anything to anyone, because no one is willing to be a receiver. One more example: Imagine when someone gives you ten dollars. Then, you give them ten dollars back. What would the giver think of later? If I were to be the giver who gave you the ten dollars, and if I got the ten dollars right back from you, I would not bother to give it to you again, any other time. Why? Because I would think that I just wasted my effort, feeling, energy, and time in giving you something that you showed that you didn't appreciate, by rejecting it and giving it back to me.

When I was still in college, I loved to wear suits to my study session; it made me feel amazing inside; it made my self-confidence increase; it made my self-esteem increase; it made me love myself very much because of the attention I got from the people around me; and it made me felt charismatic, just as my name suggests, because I thought I was the first, best, and most unique, when I wore that suit.

Nevertheless, because I was the only one who wore suits during that time, it made me look very different from anyone else around me. I always got praises along these lines: "Hey, you look great in that suit!" "You sure want to live up to your name." "Do you have any presentations for today? Because you look terrific!"

When I was having my internship during my final semester in my college years, I still wore suits to work, and I still got the same kind of praises from most of my colleagues whom I met at the office. But what distinguished me from some people when getting praises was that I replied to them only with "Thank you," each time, and then I walked away. I did praise other people too, but only when I really meant it and when I thought that it was okay for me to do so.

When you accept praises with only *thank yous*, you will look confident in the eyes of other people. You will make the giver feel good about themselves. You will become better and better in accepting praises. You will send the message to God that you are accepting what He gives you, and you will attract more of it. And by the time you realize it, you will have much more of what you are grateful for.

The More You Give, The More You Will Get

Being grateful is not always about getting. It's about giving too. Actually, we get more when we give. Winston Churchill said, *"We make a living by what we get. We make a life by what we give."*

My marketing trainer, Jay Abraham, who is well known for introducing the marketing funnel, once said, *"Value is not what we get. It's what we give."* What I understand from this quote from him is that if you want to increase your own value, you must give it first. The more value you give, the more value you will get, which leads to you making more money.

I heard something quite similar from one of my online business empire trainers, Peng Joon. He said that in order to get money from your bank account, you have to put money in it first. If you don't put any money in it, how are you going to withdraw any money from it? The same thing applies to value. You must put in the value first before you can get it back.

Ben Carson said, *"Happiness doesn't result from what we get, but from what we give."* This looks like giving can be applied to the concept of happiness too. This is very true. Sometimes you can only find your true joy in life by giving.

Be the Best Student

Imagine that you are rich, and you know some family who is very poor, and sometimes they don't have enough money to buy food for themselves. Then, you stretch out your hands to help them by giving them some money for them to buy food, and by teaching them how they can make some money. Later, when you know that they are able to make money from the ways that you've taught them, how would you feel at that moment? It feels wonderful, right?

Imagine that you have a box of chocolates. Initially, you can have it all to yourself. Of course you can, it's yours anyway. But, when you share it with your family or friends, you will then know and understand that when you share it with other people, it will taste even better, and you will want to eat it with them even more.

One of the facts that I get from giving is: If you give one, you will get ten in return. Here's my story: I once met a woman who had a company that sold homemade snacks. I met her during one of the seminars I had attended before. During the seminar, she brought one of the snacks that she was selling in her store. The snack was packed in a jar.

The woman gave the people around her the chance to taste her snack. At that time, I didn't think much about its taste. To my surprise, the snack tasted very good, and I told her about what I was thinking at that time. It was my immediate reaction in the spur of the moment. She seemed very delighted hearing what I had just said. At the end of the seminar, I got to meet her again. This time, she gave me a whole new jar of the same snack she got me to taste before. I thanked her for that. Quite some time later, I decided to order ten jars of the same snack from her—the woman gave me only one jar, but later, she had a buyer for ten jars of it.

Being grateful is also about giving. When you give something, you will get more of what you give. Start giving today, and see how your life changes for the better.

Be Grateful to Yourself

The top performers are always grateful to themselves, as they know, without their own willpower and ability and their style of thinking, they would not have become the person they are right now. They know that they are their own reasons for why they are where they are right now. They obtain all of those based on their own past experiences, what God has given them all their life, what they deduced based on their thinking, and they act accordingly upon those things.

When you are grateful to yourself, you will take great care of yourself. You will savor every moment of your life to its fullest. You will take care of yourself as though you are the most valuable and the dearest person available on this earth. You will take every opportunity that you can see that is possible to move you further.

When you are grateful to yourself, you will eat healthy foods for the sake of preserving yourself. You know that you are valuable, and you will want to allow yourself to live as long as possible. You understand early on that no one will do so for you and no one will help you to live for as long as possible, except for yourself. You will eat small meals, six times a day, for the purpose of maintaining your energy level all the time.

When you are grateful to yourself, you will do exercises frequently. You will keep yourself fit most of the time. You will do at least twenty minutes of exercise each day to keep your body energized, keep your heart healthy, and keep your brain oxygenated. You will keep exercising each day to preserve your health, as you understand that health is one of the greatest gifts of life that most people always take for granted. As Gene Tunney said, *"To enjoy the glow of good health, you must exercise."*

You will read, learn, and grow a lot when you are grateful to yourself. This is because you will always find a way to increase your self-worth and self-knowledge, and improve your abilities all the time. Because you are grateful to yourself, you will want to think better of yourself from time to time. You will want to increase your earning ability from time to time so that you will be able to enjoy your life more. You will use your ability to its fullest so you can feel the excitement from it.

How can you stay grateful to yourself most of the time? What you can do is, every day, after you wake up in the morning, thank God for keeping you alive, because He is the one who takes care of you and prevents any danger from harming you when you are sleeping.

And then, when you wake up, commit to do your very best, to the best of your ability and knowledge for the day. Live your day to the fullest. How many days do you have to live your life? Is it up till the moment you are living that you can live your life? No. You only have one day to live your life, which is only today. Why? Because you can't live in yesterday as it has become your history, and because you can't live in tomorrow, because you never know if tomorrow will still be available to you. What you only have is today.

The best people live their days to their maximum abilities, and that's why they take great care of themselves by eating healthy foods, doing exercises, learning, reading, and growing a lot, because they know that without themselves, they are no one.

Take Full Responsibility For Your Life

Being grateful is also about taking full responsibility for your life. By doing this, it shows that you accept fully what God has given you. It shows that you have the ability to take control of your life. It shows that you have the awareness that you are solely responsible for what happens to you and around you. You can develop the habit of taking full responsibility for your life by completing the *90-Day Best Student Conditioning Program* that you can get at www.TheBestStudentBook.com.

Remember, you will get more of what you are grateful for. When you are grateful to yourself, you will get more of what you want and what you've acknowledged. You will stop blaming other people for what happens in your life and for what happens around you, because you understand that by doing so, you accept what God has given you.

When you take full responsibility for your life, every time something gets to you, or happens around you, or gets to your knowledge, you will say to yourself that you are responsible. Even if something happens that isn't directly because of you, such as the natural disasters that happen around you, you are still considered to be responsible, based on how you process the information in your thinking and how you act or react to it. You will feel a sense of power flowing in you. You will stop blaming other people for whatever happens to you. As a result, you will stop being angry and will manage to get a hold of yourself and your feelings.

High emotion yields low intelligence. When you take full responsibility for yourself, you will stop blaming other people, thus preventing you from getting angry or getting highly emotional. When you can control your emotion, you will be able to control your intelligence, thus allowing you to think correctly and take actions based on your values instead of based on your feelings, and, by doing so, you avoid having any regrets later on.

Accepting full responsibility for yourself is downright selfish. This is because when you accept responsibility, you don't think of anyone else but yourself. You prohibit yourself from blaming other people, but you don't blame yourself either. You do so only to allow yourself to reclaim your composure, understanding, and self-control. Rather than having negative feelings such as unworthiness or annoyance, you accept full responsibility for yourself, allowing yourself to feel relaxed and positive most of the time.

Whenever you feel negative because of what happens to you or around you, tell yourself that you are responsible, and then ask yourself, "What's important here?" Continue asking yourself the very same question until you get to isolate only one answer that is positive and will contribute to the success of what you do. Sometimes you may feel angry at your pet because it takes a dump in your house, but when you think about what is important to you at that moment, you may answer yourself that what's important here is that your pet is alive and well. You will start to think rationally, and eventually you will get the answer like a flashbulb lighting up in your head.

The thing is, accepting full responsibility for yourself is mainly about how you respond to anything that happens to and around you, because your world, and what you see, is defined by how you think about them. As Anthony Robbins said, *"Nothing in life has any meaning except the meaning you give it."* When you think of them positively, you will get positive things.

PUTTING IT ALL TOGETHER

Here it is. Congratulations on making it to the end! I'm so proud of you because not everyone has the ability to finish reading a book. Everyone can start to do anything, but not everyone can manage to do it until the end. But you just proved to yourself that you are able to finish reading this book. Once again, congratulations! You are a finisher!

In A Nutshell

In the very first chapter, I've written about why I write about the best student. All our lives, we've been a student. But, the best students are the ones who are able to unlock their hidden potentials for accomplishment and performance.

In step one, I wrote about the importance of learning what you love. I wrote about what you can do to find your passion. I wrote about how you can learn the easy way instead of the hard way like most people do.

In step two, I wrote about the *Cashflow Quadrant* by Robert Kiyosaki, and why you need to be in the right-hand side of the quadrant. I wrote about what a system is, and how you can apply it in your business, investment, or your daily lives.

In step three, I wrote about why you should associate with the best people. You can associate with them by marketing and branding yourself so that they get to know you. You should choose your friends as it will determine your income in the next five years.

In step four, I wrote about why you should want to be optimistic. It is about thinking positively and of the future most of the time. It is about keeping calm in all situations. I wrote about the *Law of Attraction* and how you can apply it for your benefit. I wrote about how you can stay positive, despite all the problems that you have or will have.

In step five, I wrote about self-confidence, which means the act of trusting yourself for your own ability, action, and decision. I wrote about its effects in your life if you were to practice it. I wrote about what you can do to have self-confidence. I wrote about the need for you to overcome your fears for success. I wrote about what you can do to make your goal clearer and more achievable.

In step six, I wrote about how to outperform your competitors, and why they are inevitable. I wrote about how you are your own business. I wrote about why winners only focus on winning. I wrote about how to identify your competitors. I wrote about clarifying your purpose of competition. I also wrote about how planning ahead can save you so much time in executing it.

In step seven, I wrote about developing the ability to be a lifelong student, and how you can advance more in your life by taking advantage of that ability of yours. Read books, go to seminars, and learn from successful people, for your own advantages.

In the bonus step, I wrote about expressing your gratitude and how you can use it to get more of what you want. Always say thank you to God and yourself, and the people around you, to express your gratitude. You will get more in return later.

Be the Best Student

The New Car Story

I once heard a story about a successful man who dreamt of buying a new car. So, he visualized himself having an Audi—a bright red Audi with a 5-liter engine, muscular and sporty looks, leather interior, full electronic system, and so on. He once saw some other person who was way younger than him, who had the very same car as the one he dreamt of, making him felt jealous about it.

One day, he was determined to go to the nearest Audi showroom just to take a look at the car that he dreamt about all these years. His intention was to only take a look at it and test-drive it. So, he went to do so and felt amazing that he was able to drive his dream car. After he finished his test drive, the car salesperson made an offer. The salesperson said, that if he were to buy the car with cash immediately that day, he would get a fifty percent discount. The offer was outrageous! Thus, the man pulled out his debit card and paid for the car immediately, and he got to drive his dream car home.

Now, he had this beautiful Audi, and when he took it for a drive on the highway, it felt like a speedboat on the sea. When the gas pedal was stepped on, it would pick up speed and go faster and faster. He was so very pleased with his new car that he got speeding ticket, after speed ticket, even on the same day, because of driving too fast, and for some reason there were too many highway patrols on the highway that day.

One day, he remembered that he had never serviced that new car after he brought it out of its showroom. So, he sent it to his friend, Marc, who was also his trusted car mechanic, to service that car. A few moments after he sent his car for servicing, Marc called him and said, "Hey, I found a problem with your carburetor. It seems that it's been hampering your car's acceleration for quite some time."

And the man said, "Well, I really never noticed that, because since the first time I drove it, it certainly works and speeds up very well and quite fast." Marc replied with, "Even so, we have to replace its valve so that it will not affect your car's engine later on, but it will cost you about seventy-eight dollars. Is that okay with you?" The man replied, "Well, sure. If it means that my car will be better afterwards, then I've got nothing to lose." So, Marc changed the valve in the carburetor of the car. Later on, the man found out from Marc that from the previous repair of the car, the valve in the carburetor was installed backwards. So, instead of the fuel bursting out into the engine like it should, it was condensing. But, even with an expensive car like an Audi, it was still okay. And then, Marc said, "I think it will have more power now, so be careful."

The man then got his car key back. Marc had parked the car in his workshop's parking lot. There was a road in front of the car, which was the exit way from the parking lot. The man would normally step on the gas, and the car would pick up power and speed, and then it would start to accelerate. But, this time, when the man stepped on the gas like usual, the car lurched to the front so fast that he had to slam on the brake immediately just to stop the car from doing so. The man couldn't believe it because Marc said that it was only a small part in the car.

Sometimes just by changing one small part in your life, you can immediately cause it to change. Your goal should be to do anything that you can so that your life can lurch to success, just like the car lurched to the front after it was serviced.

Take Action

For everything that you've learned, you must take action from it. Only then will your life change for the better. Most people learned a lot of things and said things like, knowledge is power, and other sorts of things, but despite all of the sayings, they themselves still stay in their current situation, with no improvements, even after they've read lots of books and went to lots of seminars. To assist you to take action in the lessons stated in this book, I encourage you to complete the *90-Day Best Student Conditioning Program* that you can get at www.TheBestStudentBook.com.

What I've learned from that experience is that knowledge is power, but action gets things done. You can have all the knowledge that you want, but, without taking action on it, you will not be able to get any benefit from the knowledge that you acquired. It is like if you have a present to give to your friend, but you don't give it to him/her. You definitely know that you have a present for him/her. You know it, and it equals to knowledge. But, if you don't give it to the person you want to give it to, what's the use of having it for him/her then? The act of giving it to its recipient is the action.

Thus, if you have a present for your friend, just give it to him/her so that you can show him/her that you value him/her. The same thing applies to knowledge. If you have knowledge of something, apply it so that you can show God, who gives you the knowledge, that you value it and you are grateful for what He gives you.

I've been to quite a number of seminars. I've read quite a number of books. I've listened to quite a number of audio programs. But one thing I notice that I lack right here, is taking actions. I have all the knowledge that I want from those seminars and books and audio programs, but I don't take action from it, and then I'm wondering to myself, "Why am I not making a lot of money after all of the seminars I've gone to?"

Bradley Whitford, the American film and television actor, once said, *"Infuse your life with action. Don't wait for it to happen. Make it happen. Make your own future. Make your own hope. Make your own love. And whatever your beliefs, honor your creator, not by passively waiting for grace to come down from upon high, but by doing what* you can to make grace happen... yourself, right now, right down here on Earth." Don't wait for things to happen. Don't wait for the future to happen. You are the one who creates your own future. If you let your future just happen to you—yes, you can— it will seldom be something that you always wanted.

Herbert Spencer said, *"The great aim of education is not knowledge but action."* Pablo Picasso said, *"Action is the foundational key to all success."* Action is what translates your knowledge into your reality. It is from action that you know whether the knowledge that you have is useful to you or not. You may have the knowledge on how to catch a dodo bird, but the dodo bird is already extinct—will that knowledge of yours bring you to your success now?

It is easier for you to take action if you have a schedule of small actions that leads to the accomplishment of your main goal. It will absolutely help you to see your directions clearly. I can't stress enough how important this is to your success. The bottom line is: Make your schedule of small actions that lead to the accomplishment of your main goal, follow it through, and reach your success to its end.

Self-Discipline

Even with all those actions being written, if you don't have the self-discipline to keep doing them, it will just be among the things that will have no effect on you. It is good if you start to do them, but if you don't commit to do them until you get your success, it won't get you anywhere. To discipline yourself in doing the things stated in this book, I encourage you to complete the *90-Day Best Student Conditioning Program* that you can get at www.TheBestStudentBook.com.

Self-discipline might have, by far, the most important value of all success principles; it is said that, without it, other values will not work. Self-discipline is the ability to do whatever you should do, whenever you should do it, whether you feel like doing it or not. Self-discipline is about doing things without the influence of your emotions. Self-discipline is the skill to make yourself do whatever you've promised to do, whether you want to do it or not. When you have self-discipline, you will do the things that you need or have to do, whether you want to do them or not. You will be able remove the presence of emotion in your activities so that it will not interfere with them. You will be able to score your goals faster than most people, because you can do activities without being affected by your moods and feelings. You will have the power to take charge of your life when you have self-discipline.

M. R. Kopmeyer, the author of *Here's Help*, once said something along these lines, *"The most important success principle of all was self-discipline and it was stated by Elbert Hubbard who was one of the most prolific writers in American history at the start of the twentieth century."* He then continued with, *"There are 999 other success principles that I have found in my research, but without self-discipline, none of them work. With self-discipline, they all work."*

One of the ways that you can use to apply self-discipline is that you need to at least have an action plan. An action plan is a plan that consists of a number of small goals that aim to reach your main goal. Its main aim is to make an action schedule for you to follow so that you can eliminate the existence of emotion in it, so that you can do it without the influence of your own feelings. When you can eliminate emotions from your actions, you will be able to do it continuously without your little voice affecting it.

Besides that, you may want to have someone keep you accountable for what you want to do. You can ask your friends, your family, or your relatives to keep asking you about your progress in what you want to do. I sometimes ask my friends to keep me accountable for doing something whenever I don't feel motivated for some reason. This allows me to keep doing things whenever I don't feel like it.

Furthermore, you can have self-discipline as one of your core values, and you then just need to stay true to your values. Successful people always stay true to themselves, all the time. When they say that they will do it, they will—and so can you. When you have self-discipline, you will be able to avoid one of the pitfalls to success. People with no self-discipline always say things to themselves like, "Nah, I'll just do it later," or "I feel too lazy to do it. I'll do it whenever I feel like it." But for people with self-discipline, they know that their success depends very much on how fast they finish their small tasks in order to complete their bigger goals.

Be The Best Person You Can Ever Be

Ben Carson once said, *"Do your best and let God do the rest."* H. Jackson Brown Jr. said, *"The best preparation for tomorrow is doing your best today."* Susan Beth Pfeffer said, *"The only way you can be the best at something is to be the best you can be."*

When you do and be the best that you can, and you imagine the best results out of it, God will help you to achieve what you want. Imagining your best possible outcome will tell your subconscious mind that you have already achieved whatever it is that you are imagining, and the *Law of Attraction* will kick in, and God will help you with it.

The good news is that humans are born to be rich. But how did they become poor? Unsurprisingly, they learn to be poor from their environment; they learn to be poor from their parents; they learn to be poor from their friends; and they learn to be poor from their community. They have lots of sources from which to learn how to be poor, and, unfortunately, they learn about it subconsciously, thus resulting in them being poor themselves.

People are born geniuses. But they learn not to be. Have you ever thought about why kids learn so fast and pick things up so easily when they are young? It is because they are not yet taught to suppress their imagination and their excitement of learning.

When they go to primary school, teachers tell them to stay still in their seats and control what they do. What happens then is that they subconsciously limit their imagination and excitement in learning, thus resulting in them feeling that learning is boring and unexciting. This makes them learn less about their subjects, and this may go on for the rest of their life.

In whatever you think and do, you are born with the ability to do it well. But after you're born, you are taught to do it differently than you should, to develop your talents. You can get your best ability back by unlearning what you've learned about your ability so far. It is up to you to unlearn it and to find and learn the way that works best for you.

You can also be the best person that you can be by lowering your ego and stop wanting and thinking that you're right all the time. Gerald Jampolsky said, *"You can be right or you can be happy."* Mac Attram said, *"You can be right or you can be rich, but you can't be both."* When you lower your ego and stop thinking and wanting to be right, you will be able to learn more things from the ideas of other people who always think that they need to be right. You will be able to become happy and rich because you are not attached to any of the ideas that you've thought about, allowing yourself to think of new and better ideas that can, and will, work well for you. You will feel great about yourself because you don't need to think any more about the things that will not work for you.

Commit today to be the best person that you can ever be. It doesn't really matter what other people think about you, as long as what you do is true to your own set of values, and is positive. The bottom line is, you want to be rich and happy. When you become the best person that you can ever be, opportunities will swarm to you like ants swarming the sugar, and you will become happy, rich, and successful in no time.

Harry Houdini, the Great Escape Artist

I would like to end this book with a magnificent story that I heard about Harry Houdini. He was the greatest escape artist in history and would capture the attention of media from all over the world whenever he performed. About ten decades ago, he got a challenge from the Isle of Man. The Isle of Man is located on the coast of England, and it had just built the most unescapable lockup in the world at that time.

So, the Brits issued a challenge for Harry to try to get out of their brand new lockup. Harry had no choice but to accept the challenge because it was already widely known by the media all over the world. Besides that, there was a 50,000 dollar prize— which would now be worth more than one million dollars—to be won if he proved that he was able to get out of the said lockup. But, if he were to decline the challenge, or if he were to forfeit in the middle of the challenge, he would lose the 50,000 dollar prize, along with his top-of-the-world reputation that he'd earned through his lifetime.

Harry was a locksmith when he was still a kid, and he had made a series of tiny tools that he then used to pick those locks. He had developed a way of hiding that set of tools somewhere on his body so that he could use it whenever he wanted. During the day of the challenge, the Brits stripped Harry down to his underwear, and they said to Harry that he only had one hour to get out of the lockup. After the Brits had left him alone in one of the chambers of the lockup, he then pulled out his tools from his secret place, and he went to work. He looked at the lock and he thought that it should be alright, as the lock combinations seemed familiar to him, so he put his tools in it and worked on it. He twisted the door lock and it went, "Click-a-chunk!" The locked door wouldn't open.

So, he turned all the locks back to their original position again, and he tried again. It went, "Click-a-chunk!" Once again, the locked door wouldn't open. He did the same things, again and again, but with no result at all; he still couldn't open the locks. The time started to go by very fast. He tried lots of different ways to unlock the door, but still with no result. He was sweating; his hands were slippery from his own sweat, and he was standing in a pool of it. He was trying desperately to get out of the lockup. In the end, when the clock had 60 seconds left, Harry realized that he couldn't open the locked door in front of him. He felt defeated. He was very tired. He was sweating like crazy. He fell against the locked door, and, surprisingly, the door just swung open.

It was never locked from the very beginning. What the Brits had done was that they put Harry in the lockup without actually locking its door. They just rattled the keys at the door locks. When Harry went to work to *unlock* the door in front of him, he was certain that the Brits had locked the door. So, every time Harry tried to unlock the door, he actually locked himself back in. The reality was, the door had never been locked.

The reality right now is: Your doors are not locked either. They have never been locked since early on. What actually prevents you from getting, and having, the success that you want, is your very own mind. When you realize this, you will have the single, greatest key to unlock your hidden potential for accomplishment and performance. Everything is, and will be, possible for you, as long as you think so. So, go out and be the very best student that you can ever be for your entire life. Thank you very much.

BONUS

BONUS #1: How to do dropshipping so that you can start your online business immediately without the need of any capital

BONUS #2: How to identify your primary sense in order to utilize it in helping you learn and communicate easily and better

BONUS #3: How to perform gap analysis so that you know how to get where you want to be in the future

BONUS #4: Goal setting template to use so that you will always have a guide to making clear goals

BONUS #5: 90-Day Best Student Conditioning Program to assist you to be the best student that you can ever be throughout your life

GET THEM ALL AT
www.TheBestStudentBook.com

ABOUT THE AUTHOR

Kharisma Khalid is an author, entrepreneur, trainer, president, and student. He has received direct trainings from Mac Attram, Alex Mandossian, Courtney Smith, Blair Singer, Jay Abraham, Kevin Green, Andrew Lock, JT Foxx, Sandy Jadeja, Larry Loik, Peng Joon, and many more big names in the success industry. He has received the Award of Excellence from his college during his college years for his renowned achievements. He has helped people from around the world to get what they want in their lives. Through a mixture of education, mindset, communication, marketing, and business skills training, Kharisma has become one of the key persons in helping people to get what they want in their lives by empowering them to utilize their own hidden potentials for accomplishment and performance. For more information on Kharisma Khalid, visit www.KharismaKhalid.com

www.ingramcontent.com/pod-product-compliance
Lightning Source LLC
Chambersburg PA
CBHW050912160426
43194CB00011B/2375